DOCT

DOCTORS AND TORTURE

Resistance or Collaboration?

Amnesty International French
Medical Commission
and Valérie Marange

Introduction by Charles Glass

Translated by Alison Andrews

BELLEW PUBLISHING
London

First published by Editions La Découverte, Paris, 1989

© Editions La Découverte, Paris, 1989
All rights reserved
This edition first published by Bellew Publishing Company Ltd 1991

Bellew Publishing Company Ltd
7 Southampton Place, London WC1A 2DR

ISBN 0 947792 56 2

Printed and bound in Great Britain by
Billing & Sons Ltd

Contents

The authors wish to pay tribute to the contribution made to this book by Dr John Dawson of the British Medical Association. Dr Dawson, who died in December 1990, was a committed proponent of the role of the doctor as a protector of human rights and was a chair of one of the working parties at the meeting 'Medicine at Risk: the doctor as human rights abuser or victim' on which this book is based.

Author's note

It would be impossible to list here all the people who have contributed to this book. The greater part of the material has its origin in an international conference organised by the French Medical Commission of Amnesty International in January 1989 in Paris. The theme of the conference was 'Medicine at Risk: the health professional as abuser or victim' (see the Appendix for a list of participants and the text of the recommendations of the conference).

The theme of the conference has, in fact, been the subject of consideration for many years, particularly by the medical groups of Amnesty International in addition to their practical activity, and also elsewhere, by other associations and in various publications.

The present work has therefore drawn on various sources. This is why Amnesty International cannot be held liable for the book's contents which touch on matters quite outside the scope of that organisation. Nor does this book claim to reflect fully the Paris conference. It is hoped that it presents a synthesis as complete and accessible as possible of the reflections of individuals and groups on medical ethics and human rights.

The French Medical Commission of Amnesty International has provided the catalyst for the book. It has been co-ordinated and written by Valérie Marange.

Introduction to the English edition

(*Captain Segura:*) '*Dr Hasselbacher does not belong in the torturable class.*'

   '*Who does?*'

   '*The poor in my own country, in any Latin American country. The poor of Central Europe and the Orient. Of course in your welfare states you have no poor, so you are untorturable. In Cuba the police can deal as harshly as they like with émigrés from Latin America and the Baltic States, but not with visitors from your country or Scandinavia. It is an instinctive matter on both sides. Catholics are more torturable than Protestants, just as they are more criminal . . .*'

Graham Greene, *Our Man in Havana* (Heinemann, 1958)

Most people, however much they disapprove of torture, can imagine circumstances under which they would recommend its use. If a criminal in police custody knew the exact time and location that a bomb he had just planted would explode, killing hundreds of innocent people, the police might well be justified in using torture to obtain the information when all other means failed. Who would accuse them of having committed an unspeakable evil? Who would act to prevent them? If the police were to insist a physician be present during the interrogation, to minimise the long-term ill-effects of the torture, would the physician be right or wrong to attend?

When circumstances are slightly different, answers to these questions become more problematic. Imagine that the man who knows when and where the bomb will go off is not a criminal. He knows by chance that the bomb will go off, but he has been told that his own family will be killed if he reveals the bomb's location. Would the police be right to use torture, if all persuasion failed, on this man? Would a physician be right to refuse to participate, when he would be able to prevent permanent damage to the interrogee?

When torture is used by the State as a matter of course to obtain information, to punish and to intimidate its own population, most people would agree that its use is wrong. They would state also that doctors ought not to participate in the evil that is done to torture victims. The use of torture – both physical and psychological – is increasing, particularly in third world military and police dictatorships. Torture is used, not so much to save lives, as in the case of the man who knows where the bomb is, but to destroy lives, to make people afraid, to eliminate dissent and free discussion, and to preserve the privileged access of the few to the wealth of a country.

Although it would seem clear to most people that doctors who assist in torture are violating their Hippocratic Oath, the doctors themselves do not always see their actions as a breach of their duty to protect life. Some believe they are saving lives, albeit those of people who are not in the torture chamber, and preserving their societies from changes they fear will make life worse. Some, like the doctors who worked at Auschwitz for the Nazis, assist in torture and murder to save their own lives. In his *Survival in Auschwitz* (Macmillan, 1961), Primo Levi described the level to which the camp medical staff had been reduced: 'Everyone knows that it is the nurses themselves who send back on the market, at low prices, the clothes and shoes of the dead and of the selected who leave naked for Birkenau; it is the nurses and doctors who export the restricted sulphonamides to Buna, selling them to civilians for articles of food.'

There are two world views that would, except in extreme cases, appear to be diametrically opposed: one posits that torture is permissible as a means of social control, the other that torture is not. In order to decide which view to hold oneself, it would make sense to imagine two worlds: one in which torture is normal and another in which it is prohibited. The world in which torture is a normal part of life is not so distant from the reality of the Nazis in Germany, the Stalinists in the Soviet Union and its satellite states, the military dictatorships of Latin America, the early years of the Suharto regime in Indonesia, the final years of French rule in Algeria, the interrogation centres in the Israeli-occupied territories and life in modern Iraq under Saddam Hussein. It is a world that has debased human beings, reduced them to creatures afraid of their rulers and of one another. The torturer's electric shocks replace rational debate.

Torture often destroys individuals who survive it. Frantz Fanon, whose work as a psychiatrist under the French in Algeria is recorded in his *The Wretched of the Earth* (Grove Press, New York, 1963), described different categories of torture and the effects on the victims. After 'so-called preventive tortures of an indiscriminate nature,' Fanon encountered patients who had '(a) Agitated nervous depression . . . (b) Loss of appetite arising from mental causes . . . (c) Motor instability . . .

'Two feelings seemed to us to be frequent in the first category of tortured people:

'First that of suffering *injustice*. Being tortured night and day for nothing seemed to have broken something in these men . . .

'Secondly, there was indifference to all moral arguments. For these patients, there is no just cause. A cause which entrains torture is a weak cause . . . Force is the only thing that counts.'

In the second category, those tortured with electricity, Fanon found 'Localised or generalised coenesthopathies . . . "pins and needles" throughout their bodies; their hands seemed to be torn off, their heads seemed to be bursting, and their tongues felt as if they were being swallowed . . . apathy, aboulia, and lack of interest . . . (and) electricity phobia.' Fanon found similar long-term symptoms among those who underwent treatment with sodium penthothal, the so-called 'truth serum', and brainwashing. Many of those who underwent torture in Algeria were unable to sleep normally and their hair turned white. Some men became impotent, and women were unable to menstruate. The short, sharp shock of torture became for them a life sentence.

In an imaginary world where torture is not permitted, social control relies on consent or on less brutal means of coercion. With exceptions, many of which are noted in this book, most of the Western world has abandoned the use of torture within its own borders. Although some soldiers may torture suspects in Northern Ireland and some policemen may beat prisoners in the United States of America, such behaviour is not the norm and is not endorsed in law. The world that rejects the torture of human beings is one that respects the integrity of the individual, one that refuses to make man the object of other men, one in which my strong suspicion is that most people – given the choice – would prefer to live.

Most people do not have the choice. Those who happened to be in Santiago in 1973, when the Chilean military overthrew the elected government, did not volunteer to enter the sports stadium where the murders and torturing took place. Nor did they choose the system of government that came out of those bloody days, although Chile stands on the brink of a restoration of democracy and most Chileans have rejected forever the right of their State to torture them. The peasants of Guatemala and El Salvador, who have been brutalised by death squads and military torturers, had no choice about the type of society they wanted. Indeed, those who express their preference for change are tortured and killed. The people of Eastern Europe have made a choice, and they have decisively rejected the world of midnight arrests, internal spying and State torture. Some day, perhaps, the people of Latin America, Africa and China may have the chance to make the same decision.

The physician who participates in torture helps to perpetuate systems that degrade the victim and the torturer. Fanon recounted the case of a police inspector who came to him for treatment because he had begun to torture his own wife and children. The policeman revealed that his work in Algeria was torture. 'The thing that kills me most is the torture,' he told Fanon. 'You don't know what it is, do you? Sometimes I torture people for ten hours at a stretch ... You've got to cure me, Doctor.'

Fanon found the man difficult to treat: 'As he could not see his way to stopping torturing people (that made nonsense to him for in that case he would have to resign), he asked me without beating about the bush to help him to go on torturing Algerian patriots without any prickings of conscience, without any behaviour problems, and with complete equanimity.'

States that practice torture rely on doctors to prolong the lives of victims and to preserve the sanity of torturers, so they can go on torturing 'without any prickings of conscience, without any behaviour problems, and with complete equanimity'. Doctors who perform this double function on behalf of the State must ask themselves whether this was the reason they studied medicine and whether other doctors might be needed for them to preserve their consciences and equanimity during and after participating in torture. In some places, however, doctors face a choice between participation and death. Some of these healers may, in small ways and from time to time, alleviate suffering and quietly assure the torture victim that he is not alone. It is a difficult task and, for some, death is the easier choice.

The documentary evidence published annually by Amnesty International, Human Rights Watch, the United States State Department in its *Report on Human Rights* and other organisations reveal the steady rise in the use of torture. The fact that more countries resort to torture more frequently is an indication that most of the world is complicit. The United States and other democracies give money and sell arms to notorious torturers. No country in the Western world can say it has no trade with torturing countries. Citizens of Western democracies have the right to demand an end to assistance to the worst offenders, but they do not.

Until 2 August 1990, the United States was supplying Iraq with $1 billion in annual agricultural credits and another $250 million in Export-Import Bank loan guarantees to purchase American high technology equipment. The United States sent its navy to the Gulf in 1987 and 1988 to protect the Iraqi Government from Iran. The US was Iraq's major trading partner. Western Europe maintained cordial relations with Saddam Hussein's government, and European companies provided him with much of the dual use technology that was found, on Iraq's invasion of Kuwait, to have one use only, and that a military one. The Soviet Union was Iraq's main arms supplier and benefactor.

Iraq meanwhile tortured and murdered its citizens with regularity. It deployed weapons in violation of agreements that it would not do so. It used the poison gasses on Iranian troops, on Iraqi army deserters and on Iraqi Kurdish civilians. It built security and interrogation centres, where both adults and children were tortured. In the United States, Western Europe and the Soviet Union, the revulsion against Iraq's behaviour was insufficient to bring an end to world support for Saddam Hussein's government. In the US, business groups such as the US-Iraq Business Forum lobbied Congress to assist Iraq, invited businessmen and legislators to Baghdad and told the world that conditions in Iraq were improving – when they were in fact becoming worse.

Only when Iraq invaded Kuwait did the world turn against Saddam Hussein. Yet, to anyone who has studied his record and his commitment to terrorising his own population, Saddam was obviously not a man to be supported. The world helped him to create his massive army and his brutal security apparatus. Now the world is paying the price. Doctors must mend the wounded, and undertakers will bury the dead.

Although Saddam Hussein has brought upon himself the opprobrium of the world by his invasion of Kuwait, many other dictators and torturers continue to escape public attention. Much of the Western press ignores their crimes, and Western governments assist them in maintaining power over their populations. Perhaps because States such as El Salvador and Guatemala have not invaded friendly oil States such as Kuwait, they remain free to murder and abuse peasants, trade unionists and human rights activists within their borders. Any physicians who live in those States are expected to assist in torture and to remain silent about death squads.

This book suggests that international solidarity among physicians may help doctors to avoid becoming accomplices in State crimes. The Turkish Medical Association, for example, insists its members file correct reports on the ill-treatment of prisoners, and in June 1989, suspended a prison doctor who neglected to include in her medical report any mention of the abuse of a prisoner. Other medical bodies are in a position to take similar action and to assist medical associations in other countries that want to prevent the use of torture. More than this, all citizens of democratic societies have the freedom to demand that their governments do not provide assistance to countries that routinely use torture. Those who do not do so are as guilty as any doctor who takes the detainee's pulse between sessions in the torture chamber.

CHARLES GLASS
Dhahran, Saudi Arabia

Preface to the French edition

by Paul Ricœur*

Those interested in recent developments in moral, juridical and political philosophy have more instruction to derive from the authors of this book than they have lessons to impart to them.

As the title suggests,† the issues explored here can be viewed as representing the two sides to the coin. The central concern of the book is the involvement of doctors (and other health professionals) in human rights violations, the extreme form of which is torture. But there are also doctors who resist torture, and the book accords to these physicians the justice which is their due. At the same time, it throws open the debate on an ethical, juridical and political level, on a type of resistance not limited to the heroic testimony of a few brave men and women, but one which would be expressed in a general determination to bring the legislation of States founded upon the rule of law closer to the idealised vision of human rights that they tend to project.

Several lessons emerge concerning the first side of the coin. The main one is that when doctors take part in torture, this is not an aberration totally unrelated to honest medical practice. Rather, it represents one extremity of a continuous scale of compromises, whose other extremity blends into 'normal' medical practice. This is where everything begins, from the moment when medical practice is reduced to a technique, which is admittedly scientific, but divorced from that ethic of concern which is sensitive to other people's suffering and respects the patient's right as a human being to life and medical care. In one sense, the medical profession as such is a

* Honorary President of the International Institute of Philosophy.
† The title in French is *Médecins tortionnaires, Médecins résistants* (Doctors who torture, and doctors who resist).

risk profession. The Hippocratic Oath binds the doctor, and all medical personnel, to exclusive concern for the patient's life and health, but this necessarily and legitimately involves techniques that objectivise the patient and give the health professions a power over other people's bodies which paradoxically derives from the concern to preserve life and treat illness. Recognising the avalanche of accelerating moral decline that involves what the book describes as 'risk situations', and locating the onset of that decline at the very heart of ordinary medical practice, constitutes a courageous act of intellectual honesty. This has its counterpart, on the 'resistance' side of the coin, in the refusal to separate medical technique from the ethics of concern, which is in itself part of the legal and political practice of human rights.

The main argument developed in the book relates to the continuity between ordinary medical practice and doctors' participation in actual torture. It examines the 'risk indicators' associated with the situations which form a link between, on the one hand, normal medical practice, based on a contract of medical care, and the opposite extreme: the conscious, willing, gleeful and sadistic participation in torture. The reader will learn a great deal from the careful critical examination of several typical situations in which falling moral standards are not simply due to avoidable professional mistakes, but also, in a certain measure, to social, legal or political structures where violence takes on forms that can fairly be called institutionalised.

The first of these structures is the psychiatric hospital, where deprivation of freedom, usually through administrative committal, is an integral part of the functioning of the institution. Here, the concern to treat the patient comes up against demands of order, security and tranquillity which conflict, in varying degrees, with that concern.

On the border between the psychiatric institution and the prison there is another risk situation, that of medico-legal (or medico-social) forensic expertise. This gives the doctor considerable power in the decision to convict and in the meting out of punishment.

Medical practice in prison is definitely a high-risk area, and the book stresses the central importance of declining ethical standards in this context. The authors have not shied away from the ambiguous nature of many situations where the duty to care for the patient comes into conflict with the rules of order involved in the very notion of punishment, and therefore inherent in the prison institution. This situation, among others, raises another essential consideration for moral philosophy: that there are situations where the norms are so uncertain that the only possible recourse is moral judgment on the spot. This consideration seems to me so important that I see in it, to use a musical analogy, the counterpoint to the main theme of continuity between the normal practice of medicine in the framework of the pact of healing and the various forms of participation in torture. The problem is first posed by the forensic expertise report, from the moment it is separated from any therapeutic intent. The violation of medical confidentiality thus becomes part of the rules of the prison game; but conversely, confidentiality can turn into the silence that covers up violations of prisoners' rights. The authors have aptly described the ambiguities and contradictions of prison medical practice as falling 'between the Devil and the deep blue sea'. The problem of a hunger strike in prison is exemplary. There is a narrow dividing line between respect for a mature and clearheaded decision by the prisoner – which invites the doctor to leave the hunger striker the choice of whether to die – and the duty to help a person in danger, which appears to entail an obligation to force-feed the prisoner. There is no general rule that can relieve the doctor of having to make a unique judgment in every case. He must decide whether the prisoner is taking the risk of dying in full awareness of all the implications of his situation, and whether, beyond a certain threshold of danger, he is still in a condition to make a reasoned judgment about an action which is essentially a non-action.

I am grateful to the authors for having placed doctors' participation in the death penalty in close proximity to these risk situations. Doctors' assistance amounts to the 'medicalisation' of the death penalty, following in the footsteps of Dr Guillotin and American experts on electrocution and lethal injections. There is another trap lurking here, the trap of the humanitarian motive which generally accompanies this medicalisation. The case is particularly flagrant when the doctor is asked to attest the prisoner's fitness for capital punishment. There is a gross contradiction between treating a patient and certifying a convict fit to die. It would appear that the only radical way out of this trap set by the good conscience is to put the death penalty itself on trial, with superior moral arguments. In the USA and a majority of other countries, the death penalty is not listed among cruel, inhuman or degrading forms of punishment. The doctor should not be using his arsenal of technical skills here, but his moral and political judgment. There comes a time when the doctor and the nurse can no longer go on hiding behind the law and soothing themselves with the security arguments that back it up. They have to be brave enough to judge the law, condemn it, and disobey it. As the book says, there is a simple choice between abolishing the death penalty and medicalising it. In any case, medicalising capital punishment calls for behaviour that contravenes medical ethics, which only recognise the duty to preserve life and treat illness. The same argument is clearly valid in the case of punitive mutilations – cutting off hands and feet, and various excisions – when the executioner would seldom be able to operate without the expertise of a doctor to carry out 'clean' mutilations. The humanitarian argument resurfaces here, with its pernicious logic.

In fact, medicalisation of punishment, with its pseudo-moral justifications, was already on the silent agenda of the risk situations mentioned earlier: prisons and psychiatric institutions. The often disguised relationship between these two situations is brought out into the open by the punitive use of psychiatry, as was the case in the Soviet Union in the past (and probably still is), and under other totalitarian or authoritarian regimes. In a sense, the punitive use of psychiatry also constitutes a form of medicalisation of punishment, since an *ad hoc* nosology plays the same screening role as humanitarian arguments do for degrading forms of punishment.

Closer and closer, this brings us back to torture. The book provides many lessons on the involvement of doctors and other health professionals, and these are perplexing. First, there is the fact that the lower threshold of torture is not easy to identify. The authors were right to devote the first chapter to the problem of the anti-terrorist struggle in the United Kingdom. Although the UK has put a stop to attempts to legitimise unacceptable treatment in the pursuit of information, the problem still exists at global level, of how to discern the threshold that separates torture from the violence justified in terms of legitimate punishment. It is important to note that torture begins with *isolation*. The effects of isolation on destructuring the personality should be clearly identified and denounced (the problem is compounded by prolonged standing, hooding, exposure to constant noise, and deprivation of food or drink). The struggle against terrorism reveals the vulnerability of medical ethics to repressive policies. Here we recall what has already been said about the humanisation and trivialisation of torture, which are reflected in many anti-terrorist laws. It becomes all the more important to extend the definition of torture and make it more precise. The physical aspects of torture ought not to mask its true nature, which is mental destruction: destruction of the personality through loss of self-respect, aiming for humiliation which can sometimes be worse than death. We need to know – or guess at – the depths of torture, if we want to be clear about the progression towards moral decline mentioned above. An extermination camp survivor such as Primo Levi, who is often quoted in the book, can convey something of the *horror* of torture to a public who have grown blasé about 'the banality of evil'. Without the support of the written word, the horror might remain unspeakable.

I would not like to end this preface without recommending what the book has to say about doctors who resist. First of all, there are testimonies from doctors and nurses who, at the price of their own safety or even their lives, have said 'No' to torture, and to the seductive humanitarian arguments by which it is normally justified. But there is also the battle being waged in national and international law, by the World Medical Association, the World Psychiatric Association, and various human rights organisations. Resistance not only means behaving as a dissident with regard to punitive medicine, it also means awakening consciences and trying to change the law. International law in particular, as we are reminded, contains few references to medical practice in the context of human rights, and has no power of sanction against violations. One of Amnesty International's objectives is to get the death penalty and many types of corporal punishment included in the definition of torture. The provision of treatment for victims of repression – such as the International Centre for the Rehabilitation of Torture Victims, in Copenhagen – extends the efforts from the juridical and institutional level to the practical level. Quite apart from its therapeutic value, this organisation reminds everyone that 'the whole of society suffers from the illness of torture'. Faced with this situation, people should not be afraid to invoke the 'right to intervene' in any country's internal affairs, as that right is based on the universal nature of all human rights.

To conclude: medical codes of conduct must of necessity be international, and therefore operate on the juridical and, ultimately, on the political level where it is only pressure from citizens like ourselves, reading this book, that can carry forward the action of a voluntary organisation such as Amnesty International.

Foreword

Against the background of a battle waged for over a decade by professionals faithful to their ethical values, this book portrays a situation to which no one living on our planet can remain indifferent. Everyone, moreover, can exert an influence on this situation provided that he refuses to resign himself to it and is prepared to support those who fight against the unacceptable.

In this context, Non-Governmental Organisations (NGOs), which originate in the civil society of the various countries, provide individuals with the means to exercise a countervailing power of limited but real effectiveness, a power that can at times prove to be decisive.

Amnesty International, one of these NGOs, has the special merit of possessing its own research service – which is a guarantee of reliability and impartiality – and of being, at the same time, an agency providing information on certain types of human rights violation, as well as a movement of activists who are constantly on the alert to denounce and combat such violations. It is therefore in an ideal position to promote initiatives such as the conference on 'Medicine at risk: the health professional as abuser or victim',* even though the questions of medical ethics discussed there sometimes went beyond the range of Amnesty's statutory mandate.

Two salient characteristics mark the current world situation with respect to human rights. One is the extent and gravity of human rights violations, the other is the vigour and universality of the protests against them.

Physical elimination of political opponents or trouble-

* International conference organised by the Medical Commission of Amnesty International, French Section, 19, 20, 21 January 1989, UNESCO, Paris.

makers by hired killers and 'death squads' is common practice in much of Latin America, as well as in other parts of the world, such as the Philippines. In areas where national armies and security forces are fighting armed opposition movements, the civilian population often become hostages to both sides, who impose their will through terror. This can be observed in Sri Lanka and Peru.

Torture has been an established administrative practice in many countries for a long time. Innumerable accounts have reached us over the years from Iraq, Iran, Syria, Turkey, Somalia, South Africa, Afghanistan, Ethiopia, Indonesia, Chile, El Salvador, Guatemala and Panama, among others, to the effect that political prisoners are systematically tortured and deaths in detention are common.

Torture is also resorted to, although not as a constant and generalised practice, in countries such as Egypt, Algeria, Morocco, Mauritania, Zaire, the Congo, Cuba, India and South Korea. It is difficult for investigators to obtain access to countries such as North Korea and Albania, but conditions of detention are known to be frequently very harsh and prisoners are known to suffer ill-treatment, the seriousness of which, however, it is hard to assess.

In Romania, Czechoslovakia, the German Democratic Republic and Bulgaria, ideological nonconformity still leads to prison. It also sends people to psychiatric hospitals. This continues to be the case in the Soviet Union as well, despite the important changes that are taking place there.

International declarations proclaim the right to life. Yet the majority of national legislations still have capital punishment in their arsenal of penal sanctions. Executions continue to take place in nearly a hundred countries that include South Africa, Nigeria, Ghana, Iraq, Syria, the USSR, the USA, India, Japan and China.

Amnesty International is opposed to the death penalty in all circumstances. It is trying to encourage the nations where it still exists to move towards abolition, as the United Nations General Assembly invited them to do in 1971 and 1977.

The first condition that must be met in order to bring about the establishment of an order respectful of the rule of law is to ensure that the sinister realities of political violence cannot be concealed and that the powers which have resorted to such violence cannot evade their responsibilities before the court of international public opinion.

The action taken to achieve this goal has developed within the framework of a system of institutionalised intervention stemming from the United Nations Charter, which makes of any question related to human rights an international matter. It is worth recalling that it has required considerable perseverance, energy and spirit of sacrifice on the part of human rights activists, as well as coherent, methodical work on the part of the NGOs that support them, to get the principles of the Charter translated into practice. Governments have had to be convinced that, by virtue of these principles, they are accountable to the international community for the way they guarantee fundamental individual rights. They have had to be persuaded to accept the legitimacy of private initiatives, individual or collective, to defend these rights.

Progress since 1975, the year of the Helsinki agreements, can be measured by what took place in Vienna in January 1989, when the signatory States formally undertook to guarantee their citizens 'the right to contribute actively, individually or in association with others, to promoting and safeguarding human rights and fundamental freedoms'. For the 'Helsinki Watchers' and East European dissidents, this was recognition from the very people who had persecuted them pitilessly for years. Of course their battle is not over yet, but they have gained a much broader audience and a wider scope for action, and this recognition is an important step towards strengthening the international system for safeguarding human rights.

This advance is part of the general progress in the participation of civil society in the development of the legal protection of human rights.

The advent of individuals and private organisations to the sphere of international law, previously reserved to States alone, has been given official sanction through their right of recourse to supranational jurisdictional and quasi-jurisdictional bodies, as well as through the consultative status granted to NGOs *vis-à-vis* the United Nations Economic and Social Council. The organisations with sufficient means to fulfil this role can influence the development of human rights policies. They contribute to perfecting legal mechanisms and to establishing protective measures.

In the particular area of torture, where 'doctors at risk' are involved, Amnesty International has joined forces with other organisations such as the International Commission of Jurists and the Swiss Committee against Torture. Their joint action contributed greatly to building up the pressure of opinion that culminated in the adoption by the UN General Assembly of the convention of 1984, and in the Geneva Commission's appointment of a special rapporteur on the perpetration of acts of torture. Like his colleagues who deal with other serious violations of human rights, this rapporteur works on the basis of information supplied almost entirely by NGOs.

This review of progress is not intended to promote a favourable opinion of NGOs, but rather to overcome the temptation to feel sceptical and discouraged about the current state of the world. It serves simply to confirm that all the professionals, jurists, journalists and human rights activists who came to the Paris conference, sometimes from great distances, were right to believe in the virtues of solidarity and collective action. The organisations and teams they work in have remarkable accomplishments to their credit, which, steadily improved upon, will each day bring the UN principles a bit closer to practical reality.

But it is important to remember that in this area nothing is ever definitely won. Vigilance can never be relaxed, and the support networks have to stay in a permanent state of alert. This implies constant effort: to keep all the strands of the network firm and efficient, to sensitise public opinion and gain public support, and to assess correctly the situations to be dealt with, and understand their political, cultural and emotional dimensions.

The battle for human rights must be planned with care, guided by mature reflection. This is why those involved need to meet and share their experiences. 'Learning how to take an ethical stand means first learning about doubt', as Valérie

Marange says in Chapter 10, and the comments by doctors whom she quotes clearly illustrate the point. These physicians, wherever they work, know that their daily occupations expose them to ethical problems which have no ready-made solutions in the professional code of conduct. The art of controlling one's conduct (which is a definition of ethics) can only be practised in the context of the concrete situation. In every case it is personal judgment that will shape the attitude to be taken, in line with the fundamental dictates of conscience.

The events that have marked Europe in the twentieth century, and are still occurring today in this global village of ours, show that humanism is daily at war with nihilism. And the decisive choice is taken in individual consciences. The 'doctors at risk' in Paris were modest and courageous witnesses to that choice.

We may justifiably have our doubts about what constitutes the Good, since far too many Utopias have bloodied the world in the name of political or metaphysical truth. But we can have no doubts about what is Evil, because events have taught us all about it.

AIMÉ LÉAUD, jurist,
former President of the French Section
of Amnesty International

1 Putting a 'human' face on torture

Barely twenty years ago in Western Europe, torture was almost declared legal, provided it was justified by a political situation and carried out under medical supervision.

This happened in the United Kingdom in the early 1970s. The British press in 1971 reported accounts by witnesses of physical brutality against prisoners suspected of belonging to the IRA, during their interrogation by the police in Northern Ireland. In response to these allegations, two successive commissions of enquiry were set up. They acknowledged that methods of 'depth interrogation' were in use in Ulster: prolonged standing against a wall, wearing a hood over the head, subjection to continuous noise, and deprivation of food or drink. They then set out to justify these practices and define a framework of regulations that would make them acceptable.

'Strict discipline and isolation'

The first argument, citing the element of urgency in the combat against terrorism, is classic. 'Intelligence is the key to successful operations against terrorists,' says the Compton Report. 'Information can be obtained more rapidly if the person being interrogated is subjected to strict discipline and isolation.' The reasoning becomes more tortuous when it comes to proving the 'humane' nature of the techniques, and distinguishing 'discipline' and 'isolation' – the key words in this report – from 'violence' and 'humiliation', which interrogators are officially forbidden to use. The Compton Commission says there is no 'brutality' in these techniques because 'brutality is an inhuman or savage form of cruelty, and that cruelty implies a disposition to inflict suffering, coupled with indifference to, or pleasure in, the victim's pain'. It was assumed that the medical guarantees available to the detainees (examination before they were interrogated, and a daily visit from a doctor) were adequate proof that there was no indifference or pleasure involved.

The latter aspect was more heavily stressed by the Parker Commission in 1972. It enlisted medical opinion to prove the 'humane' nature of the techniques that were used: 'The risk of physical injury is negligible. That was the evidence of all the medical witnesses.' As for the consequences for mental health, 'There is no reliable information in regard to mental effects, particularly long-term mental effects, and, as one would expect, the medical evidence varied somewhat.' Yet the writers of the report dismissed the psychological after-effects as negligible, on the basis of experiments carried out in the army. In the Commission's view, nothing could be concluded from the results of tests on student volunteers even though they were quite negative, since 'in these cases the volunteers neither enjoyed a break during which medical examination and later interrogation took place, nor were they members of an organisation bound together by bonds of loyalty which would help them to hold out'. The Commission therefore concluded that 'while long-term mental injury cannot scientifically be ruled out, particularly in the case of a constitutionally vulnerable individual, there is no real risk of such injury if proper safeguards are applied'. It proposed that 'a doctor with some psychiatric training should be present at all times at the interrogation centre, and should be in a position to observe the course of interrogation'.

The humanitarian temptation

The implication was that torture can be made humane, painless and clean, carried out without undue sadism, and under medical supervision. Later events gave the lie to the Compton and Parker Commissions. One of the members of the Parker Commission published a minority report, and the Prime Minister[1] accepted his opinion and prohibited these methods. Subsequently the European Commission on Human Rights came to the unanimous conclusion in 1976 that the combined use of the four techniques mentioned above (prolonged standing, hooding, continuous noise, and deprivation of food or drink), plus sleep deprivation which was also used in Northern Ireland, did indeed constitute a form of torture. Finally, these events caused the British Medical Association (BMA) to take up the matter. The results came a few years later in the Tokyo Declaration by the World Medical Association:[2]

> The doctor shall not countenance, condone or participate in the practice of torture or other forms of cruel, inhuman or degrading procedures, whatever the offence of which the victim of such procedures is suspected, accused or guilty ... The doctor shall not be present during any procedure during which torture or other forms of cruel, inhuman or degrading treatment is used or threatened.

The official use of torture by one of the oldest democracies in the world, and by members of the medical profession, did not last long. Yet the temptation had been strong. Several years of controversy went by before the Tokyo Declaration was adopted, and even thereafter, several countries and even some doctors tried to reduce its scope on the grounds that it was too 'maximalist'. The decision of the European Commission on Human Rights concerning Northern Ireland was partially repudiated a year later by the European Court, which described merely as 'cruel, inhuman or degrading treatment' the practices that the Commission had denounced as torture. The assumption is that deprivation of sleep or the administration of a truth drug is preferable to hanging upside down by the feet, a psychiatric hospital to the gulag, and a lethal injection to the electric chair! A doctor's presence is supposed to prevent the worst, namely death or irreversible injury. Since torture is regarded as a necessary evil to save innocent persons, the horror might as well be medically controlled, as epidemics or famine are. These insidious views, recurrently expressed, illustrate the vulnerability of medical ethics to repressive policies.

Torture made commonplace ...

If such arguments could convince anyone, then or now, and such reports could be written in the Europe of the 1970s, this is because they are part of a general evolution in repressive policies, recorded at the time by Amnesty International. Despite being prohibited in 1948 by the Universal Declaration of Human Rights, torture has tended to become commonplace. In a third of the countries in the world, which may be dictatorships or democracies facing an armed opposition, torture is no longer just an aberration but an instrument of power, an established practice.[3] Of course no state officially admits to practising torture, but some of them frequently give more or less clear signs of tolerating it. All over the world, from Uruguay to Sri Lanka, and even in the Western democracies, 'security' or 'anti-terrorist' laws passed in the 1970s widen the powers of police forces and the army, and reduce the protection given to prisoners and suspects. Shadowy areas – and dangerous – have been established in institutions or on the fringes of them: there are prolonged periods of detention in police custody,[4] clandestine interrogation centres, and high-security prisons. In Turkey, the authorities still refrain from giving any clear directive to the security forces, in the full knowledge that torture is widely practised. In Guatemala, tortured bodies are exhibited and photos of them are published, to terrorise the populace. In the United Kingdom, confessions and denunciations were currently accepted as sufficient proof of guilt, even when they were extorted under duress. As torture has become more commonplace, a wider variety of personnel has become involved: various police or army intelligence services, employees in the prison service, and, in many cases, a doctor: a doctor who declares the prisoner fit to undergo the treatment, stops the torture if the victim's life seems to be in danger, sews up the wounds between one session and the next, erases the marks before a trial, declares a suspicious death to be from natural causes, and produces false certificates of good health.

... and under medical supervision

The disturbing increase of the incidence of torture around the world is linked to another tendency which has mobilised Amnesty International doctors in the past few years: the growing use of medical skill in repression. When the Compton and Parker Reports attempted to define a 'clean' form of torture that could subdue a prisoner without laying a finger on him, they epitomised the evolution that has taken place in torture in the past forty years. The involvement of medical, psychological and psychiatric knowledge in torture is so great that those who are fighting against it have had to extend and specify its definition, so as not to be deceived by its modern forms. The United Nations Declaration against torture thus includes 'acute mental suffering' in its definition, and in 1984, when Amnesty International re-launched its campaign against torture, it stressed the notion of confinement. The Compton Commission recognises solitary confinement as a way of getting terrorists to talk, and claimed to minimise its scope, but isolation is the universal basis of the torture process. Torture begins with 'strict discipline and confinement', and it represents the extreme aspect of the prison system. At least four of the five techniques used at that time in Northern Ireland – deprivation of sleep, deprivation of food or drink, hooding, and prolonged standing – are used every day by all the torturers of the world. If one object were to be taken today as a universal symbol of torture, it would be the hood. It cuts off the wearer from the outside world, isolates and depersonalises him, and stops anything existing for him – and him existing for anyone else. Whether what follows is more or less barbarous (beating or burns), or more or less sophisticated (continuous noise or psychotropic drugs), depends on local factors, mainly the degree of discretion required. Even in the most flagrant barbarity there is room for medical and technical skill, as for example in the notorious and widespread use of electric torture. Wherever torture is in use, it has a significant psychological aspect.

In many countries today legalised torture, in the form of corporal punishment or the death penalty, calls in medical assistance. In Pakistan, the law prescribes the presence of a doctor at an amputation or a flogging. In the United States, it is medical experts who define the extent to which the accused represents a danger to society, declare a convict fit to be executed, determine the lethal dose and supervise its effectiveness.

Medical ethics trapped

Torture with doctors' involvement, in the combined experience of Amnesty International and concerned doctors who today give consideration to such matters, is the result of two trends: first, a hardening of the attitude which prison and police institutions are authorised to adopt and which requires the use of more sophisticated, rational and discreet methods; second, the tendency of a certain number of doctors caught up within or on the perimeter of these institutions or even, as in the Soviet Union, within medical institutions, to adopt practices which are harmful to the patients. Medical ethics is trapped between these two trends. The resurgence of the death penalty in the United States, and the increase in corporal punishment in Islamic countries, is encouraged by the approval of the medical profession. Prison medical practice, particularly in a crisis such as a hunger strike or a mutiny, sometimes puts the doctor in the position of an accessory to repression. Forensic medicine gives the doctor considerable power in the passing and carrying out of sentences. General medical practice has high-risk areas of its own, such as psychiatric and geriatric institutions. Any place or situation in which the freedom of the patient is restricted or withdrawn, where suffering is considered normal, whose clientele is an ostracised or neglected group, and most of all if it is withdrawn from public scrutiny, will sometimes experience a decline in standards (see Chapter 2).

The involvement of doctors in judicial, prison and police methods, along with the contamination of some medical practices and institutions by certain forms of repression, is a trap set for the medical profession by the State and sometimes by the profession itself and it is nothing new. The reports of the British experience immediately bring to mind the words of the philosopher Michel Foucault[5] on the emergence in the eighteenth century of new 'technologies of power over the body' which were more discreet, less arbitrary, less painful and more scientific. The present-day involvement of doctors in the death penalty in the United States, and the construction of an amputation machine in some Muslim countries, inevitably recalls the famous device named after Dr Guillotin, who was also anxious to 'humanise' punishments. 'Clean' torture and punitive psychiatry appear as the final result of the plan for the 'deliberate manipulation of individuals' mentioned by Foucault. No doubt the jailers of Libertad (Uruguay) or the Soviet psychiatric hospitals would have agreed with the American prison inspector who spoke in 1797 about the need to 'know the principle of the sensations and sympathies that occur in the nervous system' in order to decide on the punishment.[6]

This collusion between medicine and the State resulted, in the final half of the century, in a major perversion of, and a real crisis in medical ethics. The central role played by biologists and doctors in elaborating the Nazi racial theories, and later in the selection of victims, their extermination, and the transformation of medical experimentation into torture in the concentration camps are the most visible facets of a broader tendency. 'Euthanasia' was practised on hundreds of thousands of the mentally-handicapped and mentally-ill in Germany from 1933 to 1945.[7] Tens of thousands of inmates of French psychiatric hospitals[8] were 'gently exterminated'. Biologists and doctors have taken part in eugenistic policies of forced sterilisation since the 1930s, not only in Germany but also in the United States and many other developed and developing countries. The so-called 'humanisation' of torture, capital punishment and corporal punishment must be regarded as a new element in the crisis of medical ethics.

With a clear conscience

'Humanitarian' arguments were also introduced to justify Nazi medical practices. Evidence of this appears in expressions such as 'mercy killing' (*Gnadentod*) to describe the murder of those 'unfit to live', and in the trial statement of Rudolf Höss, commandant of Auschwitz, on the development of Zyklon-B, the 'death drug': 'I have always shuddered at the thought of extermination by firing squad ... I was therefore relieved to think that we would be spared bloodbaths, and that the victims would be spared suffering right up to the last moment ...'[9] Nazi doctors, as the historian Robert Lifton relates, did not repudiate the Hippocratic Oath. It was in the name of life itself that they sanctioned or practised 'euthanasia', and perfected methods of 'clean' mass execution (see box). However these events, which should today constitute a warning against attempts to 'humanise' horror, testify to the fragility of a 'humanitarian' vision founded on purely biological or medical criteria. What these facts show is that medical sanction given before the event (selection) or after the event (execution) of a violation of human rights, provides no ethical guarantee and no mitigation of the scandalous nature of murder or torture. They show that, wherever the dignity of the person is denied, medical ethics is in peril, and that reducing humanisation to medical or biological progress, may result in a danger of perverting both ethics and humanism.

The purely technical

Perhaps the single greatest key to the medical function of the Auschwitz self was the technicizing of everything. That self could divest itself from immediate ethical concerns by concentrating only on the 'purely technical' or 'purely professional' (*das rein Fachliche*). Demonstrating 'humanity' meant killing with technical efficiency.

For the Auschwitz self there is a logical sequence: a doctor's task is to alleviate suffering and to exert a humane influence in any setting. When the setting is one of mass murder, that

Amnesty International

British Section, 99-119 Rosebery Avenue, London EC1R 4RE
Tel: 071-278 6000

The publications you have requested are:

☐ **Out of print - you will** ☐ **not be invoiced**

☐ **be credited**

☑ **Being reprinted. They will be sent when available unless you instruct otherwise.**

WIFL

means calling forth medical and technical skills to diminish the pain of victims. While the logic depends upon a highly technicized view of medical function, the Auschwitz self can grasp at the pseudo-ethical principle of 'humane killing'.

That principle was put forward not just by Auschwitz doctors but by the Nazi regime in general. Hitler himself, in his final testament-suicide note, contrasted the painful deaths of 'Europe's Aryan peoples' by hunger, battle, or bombing with the 'more humane means' by which 'the real criminal . . . [had] to atone for his guilt'.

The use of poison gas – first carbon monoxide and then Zyklon-B – was the technological achievement permitting 'humane killing'. Hence, the early advice by Grawitz, chief SS physician, when consulted by Himmler on the matter, in favor of gas chambers – surely the ultimate in such technical-medical consultation.

But these two 'humanitarians' were undoubtedly more concerned about the well-being of the killers. The psychological difficulties experienced by the *Einsatzgruppen* in face-to-face killing were also met by a form of medical technicism. The *Wehrmacht* neuropsychiatrist who had treated these psychological difficulties in *Einsatzgruppen* troops, described them to me – the general manifestations of anxiety, including anxiety dreams – in the most detached clinical tones. When I asked him whether *he* had ever experienced anxiety dreams in response to all this killing or to his treating the killers, he answered that he had not: 'I never killed anybody'; and, 'As doctors . . . we were outsiders.'

Robert J. Lifton, *The Nazi Doctors*

This is also the lesson to be learnt from the testimonies of people who have been tortured: the primary aim of torture is to destroy the mind. Via the body, the whole person and the spirit is being targeted and devastated. The factor that the Chilean *parilla* and the Turkish *falaka*[10] have in common with the administration of neuroleptics by Soviet punitive psychiatry and the psychologists in Uruguay's Libertad prison is their aim: the destruction of the person. Their own testimonies and the psychiatric reports on fourteen people subjected to the methods of the Royal Ulster Constabulary in Northern

Ireland were enough to convince the European Commission on Human Rights that torture is still torture and that it leaves marks, if not physical marks then at least psychological ones. The modern ability to destroy the self without touching the body, or to achieve the desired effect by applying less bloody forms of violence to the body, does not alter this basic fact. There is no 'humane' way of destroying a person, or that person's loyalty to himself and to others. Accounts of the degradation and suffering of prisoners on Death Row in America also underline the fact that there is no 'clean' way of killing.

The humanitarian temptation is even stronger when it comes to medical attendance during torture. 'The army hospital doctors we met in Uruguay,' says Dr Stanislas Tomkiewicz,[11] who went on a mission there in 1980, 'refused to make the connection between their intervention and torture. They said, "We aren't the ones who beat them. If there's something wrong with them, we treat them. We aren't involved in politics." They had a perfectly clear conscience.' Here again, people who have been through this kind of treatment are very clear that, to them, the doctors were torturers like the rest. The doctors would treat their wounds, often summarily, only so as to make them fit for more torture or presentable in court, and would only put a stop to the blows in order to prolong their hell.

Working towards an ethic of human rights

The fact that doctors take part in violations of human rights clearly indicates that medical ethics cannot be founded on strictly professional criteria or on a purely technical view of the doctor's vocation. Even now, in the United States, psychiatrists are involved in the sentencing to death of mentally-ill criminals who are considered 'incurable', in a sinister echo of the medical certificates that preceded 'euthanasia' in the Nazi era. This shows that the principle of respect for life, upheld by medical ethics since Hippocrates, is not an adequate barrier to the medical justification of murder. The inadequacy appears even more clearly when the prison doctor is confronted with a prisoner on hunger strike. Respect for life would mean force-feeding, but it would also mean sacrificing respect for the individual and his right to volition. Medical ethics cannot be prescribed from within the medical profession. There are inherent risks in the power a doctor derives from his medical knowledge and technical skill, and it is crucial to medical ethics that this power should be evaluated from outside the profession, from a philosophical and political point of view.

In January 1989, the French Medical Commission of Amnesty International organised a conference in Paris on 'Medicine at Risk: the health professional as abuser or victim'. Dr Umit Kartoglu, a representative of the Turkish Medical Association, spoke of the need to 'construct a new culture of human rights'. This process began in the aftermath of the Second World War, when the Nuremberg trials led to a condemnation of crimes against humanity and a code of medical ethics. This was followed by international law and papers on medical ethics. But the most important contribution to the enrichment and vitality of this law, ethics, and culture, must come from individuals, including members of medical professions. Without their constant intervention, it is always possible to slip backwards as has been proved since 1945 by numerous incidents of torture, massacres, and people being imprisoned because of their opinions. This principle, which has guided Amnesty International activists for nearly thirty years, is equally important in the realm of ethics. Without a constant questioning of medical practices, without evaluation of these practices in the light of human rights, the risk of slipping backwards cannot be ruled out. The risk arises less from any wrong application of medical ethics than from an *a priori* certainty of observing them, from a clear but blind conscience, which indicates a willingness to 'humanise' torture. The deviation is not always obvious; it often contains its own disguise. People who violate human rights always act on behalf of a good cause.

In the new ethics, respect for human dignity should be paramount, secure against all 'higher interests' and good intentions, even of a medical nature. Such ethics is first forged in practice. In South Africa, Dr Wendy Orr[12] refused to condone torture, and in the Soviet Union nurse Alexander Podrabinek[13] denounced punitive psychiatry. In the United Kingdom a few years after the events described at the beginning of this chapter, army doctors complained about the persistent ill-treatment of prisoners in Northern Ireland, and succeeded in obtaining guarantees for them.[14] Over the past ten years, in Chile, South Africa, Pakistan, Algeria, the Soviet Union, and also Denmark and France, more and more doctors and health workers have been organising resistance to practices in which others have tried to implicate them, asserting patients' rights in prisons and mental institutions, and treating the victims of repression. Their action is undoubtedly helping to reduce torture, along with the arguments that try to 'justify' it. Although the practice of medicine may involve problems, it is also an opportunity to assume one's responsibility as a citizen, by denouncing and resisting violations of human rights. Since those in power call upon their services, doctors are in a position to exert effective pressure in return. Awareness of the daily risk involved in the therapeutic relationship can make doctors into regulators of ethics and defenders of human rights.

This ethical movement, backed up by international solidarity linked to human rights organisations, has prompted widespread debate. The French Medical Commission of Amnesty International has been striving for years to promote research this field and to help to establish medical ethics based on human rights. The conference on 'Medicine at Risk' held in Paris in January 1989 was the final link in a long chain of national and international meetings, conferences and publications, which all tended in the same direction. The notion of 'risk' – the risk of serving repression, the risk of becoming its victim – was the focal point of the conference, which scrutinised ethical rules and the penalties for breaking them, and also discussed preventive action in the form of regulation and training. The purpose of this book is to record that valuable work, born of the experience of doctors and nurses from all over the world.

2 The vicious spiral, or the temptation to torture

It would be greatly reassuring to believe that all torturers were nothing but particularly brutal, illiterate persons. They are nothing of the sort, as the French public discovered when they saw Michaelis Petrou on television in April 1982. He had been a henchman of the Greek Colonels, and also happened to be a lovable father and a sensitive, cultured human being. So the torturer is not a remote monster – he could even be 'your neighbour's son'.[1] And we also now know that he could just as well be a doctor.

Michaelis Petrou did at least have the 'excuse' of being pitilessly trained and conditioned into submission. 'Tomorrow it'll be you who will give the orders and frighten other people.' Doctors involved in the torture process do not go through anything similar, and this makes their cases all the more disturbing. Such a decline in moral standards seems inexplicable in a profession trained to care for others and to do good. First-hand accounts from doctors involved in torture are rare, and do little to enlighten us. They show a series of tiny, barely perceptible lapses, which lead them from an almost normal practice of medicine into increasingly flagrant complicity.

An account published in the Brazilian press[2] by a former doctor and torturer offers an example of this gradual deterioration in ethical standards, although it provides no final 'explanation' of the phenomenon. As a young army doctor, Dr Amilcar Lobo found himself caught up in the system by means of a 'medical examination', and then by treating victims after they had been tortured. 'The commandant, Nei Fernandez, gave me a lecture on communism and then sent me to examine a prisoner. I went to the headquarters of the investigation department and saw a man of over sixty lying naked on the floor, with wires all over his body.' The man seemed to be on the point of death. The soldiers brutalised him in front of the doctor, and said, 'You see, if he was really in a bad way, he'd be dead by now. You can go, everything's fine.' Dr Lobo had not yet even touched a prisoner, but he was already implicated.

He went on treating torture victims for several years, without trying to get away and without talking about it, but with the silent complicity of his professional colleagues, especially psychoanalysts. He did not really know whether he was treating patients or taking part in torture. His motivation might have been compassion, indifference or sadism. He could not tell why he had administered electric shocks, used elsewhere as a form of torture, or why he had sutured wounds without anaesthetic. He suffered and felt schizophrenic about what he was doing, and did not know whether it was only the threats against his family that kept him from stopping. Years afterwards, Dr Lobo decided to speak out. Although he clings to 'excuses' arising from the situation itself or from experiences he had been through in his early childhood, he admits unambiguously: 'I was an accomplice in torture.' It is only this act of ethical lucidity that has enabled him to regain some kind of 'serenity' today.

'I'm only doing my job'

There must have been something that blocked Dr Lobo's awareness for so long, and prevented him taking a clear look at what he was doing. For those doctors who give in to 'the temptation to torture', as Professor Antoine Lazarus puts it,[3] what causes their blindness and passivity? Dr Lobo's story, along with data collected by Amnesty International[4] and studies on Uruguayan[5] and Nazi[6] doctors, enables us to identify a few constants. First of all there is fear, the feeling of irresistible pressure. There is often a more or less explicit acceptance of the decision to use torture. A Chilean doctor, Alfredo Jadresic, challenged a former student of his who was collaborating with the military brutality after the 1973 coup. 'What do you expect us to do?' the young doctor retorted, 'we're at war.'

There is also a narrow concept of the doctor's duty, which is experienced in a purely bureaucratic and technical way; 'I'm only doing my job,' said a Uruguayan doctor when one of his victims invoked the Hippocratic Oath.

These symptoms of lowered ethical standards are far from being unique to the medical profession. The doctor implicated in torture is primarily a very ordinary person, incapable of resisting unjust orders, ready to justify the means by the end, and quick to take refuge in a straitjacket of professionalism. 'It was a proper, definite job,' said Michaelis Petrou, 'and once I was caught up in the police system, I enjoyed doing it.'

But, in the case of the health professions, this technical attitude is shocking in numerous respects. First, it is blindly adopted in the illusion of serving a good cause, and technical good is confused with ethical good. It is all very well for a torturer who belongs to the army or police force to set himself up as a professional, but he knows that his 'profession' consists in crushing another person, even if he partially denies that person his human character. A doctor can tell himself he is fulfilling his duty by stitching up a head wound or resuscitating an injured person, as though these actions could be isolated from their context. 'This naïveté, far from being an excuse, almost amounts to an aggravating circumstance,' Professor Lazarus emphasises, since it nourishes the illusion of a more humane form of torture. The division of labour between doctors and executioners, the fact of fitting into a hierarchy, and the technical nature of their involvement, all serve to dilute responsibility and exonerate those who commit the violations.

Second, the restricted way these doctors operate is matched by a dehumanisation of the victim. Here again, it is not only the doctor who is concerned. Reducing the victim to a sub-human, the 'Communist', the 'fel',[7] the enemy, in the name of a higher interest, is a *sine qua non* condition of torture. This depersonalisation is reinforced by the physical and mental degradation imposed on the victim, which is in itself the aim of torture. But the doctor is supposed to be motivated primarily by compassion, and concern for the patient's welfare. In fact, whatever the Compton Report claims (see Chapter 1), when the only possible justification for a doctor's

presence is compassion, he is bound to slide towards insensitivity. If he identifies with the victim, he cannot possibly accept
his position. It is incredible that Dr Lobo could not understand why some of his patients committed suicide. This
attitude proves his total lack of empathy with them.

Finally, the acceptance of a higher interest than the
patient's, and the ability to reduce the therapeutic gesture
to a technical gesture, and the human person to a manipulated
body, is shocking because it is so banal. Medicalised torture
holds up a curious mirror to the imperceptible little perver-
sions of everyday medical practice. Health professionals can
become insensitive to their patients' physical or mental pain,
and reduce them to clinical cases or 'incapables' (old people,
psychotics, handicapped people). By putting the interests of
the law or financial imperatives before the welfare or freedom
of the patient, they risk giving in to that same temptation,
with the same naïve clear conscience. If doctors who torture
are not monsters, are they not in the end just ordinary doctors,
caught up in what appears as the common good, normality,
authority and technology? (See box on p. 18) Should we not
at least consider these tendencies to be risk indicators?

Risk indicators

Dr Stanley Milgram's famous experiment is very interesting
in this context. He set up a fake scientific experiment with
two groups. One group of volunteers, who were unaware that
they were taking part in a simulation, were told to test the
ability of the other group (which comprised 'actors') to
remember lists of words. They did this by giving them electric
shocks, which got stronger each time the learners made a mistake. Two out of three of the real volunteers went right to the
limit and caused the apparent death of the fake subjects. This
alarming experiment shows how far an institutional, technical
setting can undermine people's normal sense of responsibility.
But the point Milgram forgets in his interpretation of the
experiment, and which is of particular interest to us, is that
the test was supposed to be a medical one. As Dr Miguel Benasayag[8] points out, the volunteers who administered the electric

shocks were profoundly convinced that they were acting in a good cause, the cause of science. They were sure that the scientific end could justify inflicting suffering on those taking part in the experiment and that, if the experiment proved the method was effective, it could justifiably be used as a way of teaching vocabulary. The acceptance that gradually leads doctors to lower their ethical standards happens at a much earlier point than the lethal electric shocks which concluded this 'experiment'.

The Milgram experiment does not provide an explanation of torture through 'conditioning' but it does throw light on the incentives for some doctors and nurses to allow their standards to drop. In modern states governed by law and whose constitutions guarantee the integrity of the body, the medical profession is the only group entitled to contravene that principle, for the patient's own good. Any distortion of this notion of welfare can lead to all sorts of moral lapses. Hence the importance of a daily scrutiny of medical ethics.

> There are two ways of talking about human rights. The general tendency is to say that human rights are or are not being respected. But experience on the ground shows, in medicine at any rate, that things are not so clear-cut. If we want to achieve anything we have to analyse the risk indicators, that is to say the areas of our work as doctors where we are in an ambiguous position. It is sometimes possible to regulate these situations. On the other hand, if there is absolutely no way we can resist a decline in standards, we will have to learn how to turn our backs on the mess.

This is how Dr Nicole Léry, a forensic doctor in Lyons, sums up the feelings of doctors who work with Amnesty International and other human rights groups. It is not a question of referring to doctors' 'conditioning' as an excuse for taking part in torture, or of putting small lapses into the same category as major ones, but rather of using the experience of doctors who have taken part in torture to identify risk factors (see box on p. 18). The difference, of course, between these everyday risk situations and the extreme case of torture is that one can hope to do something about the former whereas there can be no 'arrangement' of torture. No one would dream of making a comparison between an act of torture and the procedure of putting a tube down a patient during resuscitation. Yet many medical staff have testified to the riskiness of the procedure, if it is carried out without due concern for the pain caused to the patient. Callousness and insensitivity are indicators of declining ethical standards and require that treatment practices be examined. More generally, in order to prevent the involvement of doctors in torture, medical practice needs to get out of the rut of naïveté and adopt a genuinely ethical approach. As Professor Jacques Védrinne says, it is important to 'maintain the most sensitive threshold of vigilance in the greatest possible number of practitioners'.[9] This, we believe, is the price to be paid in order to prevent major lapses from ethical standards.

Not murder, [but] a putting-to-sleep

Precisely that impression was vividly conveyed to me by a doctor I interviewed who had been immediately involved in the killing project: 'According to the thinking of that time, in the case of children killing seemed somehow justifiable . . . whereas in the case of the adult mentally ill, that was definitely pure murder.' Hans F. went on to tell how severely impaired the children were when they arrived ('My God . . . such high-grade imbeciles!'), that they had been insufficiently fed and were 'in terrible condition,' and how events were arranged so that the killing was not *quite* killing. The head of the institution told one of the two or three nurses colluding in the program to give the designated children luminal in their food – an order that, if not examined closely, could seem routine for impaired restless children . . .

While Dr. F. admitted that one might wonder about a child, 'Why is he sleeping so much?,' he insisted (quite erroneously) that one could ignore that inner question because 'the death rate [of those killed] wasn't much above the regular death rate with such children.' He stressed the absence of either a direct command ('If I get the order to kill . . . I don't know but I [think I] would refuse . . . but certainly there was no such order . . . for us') or of manifest homicide ('I mean if you had directed a nurse to go from bed to bed shooting these children . . . that would not have

worked'). As a result, 'there was no killing, strictly speaking
. . . People felt this is not murder, it is a putting-to-sleep.'

Of course Dr. F. sought by this kind of emphasis to justify
and exonerate himself. Indeed, the exact extent of his
culpability is not clear. He had been imprisoned for some
years while awaiting trial, had been convicted partly on
testimony that he had ordered that a child be given a fatal
dose, but his case had been appealed and eventually
dismissed, apparently for political reasons, at a time of
considerable laxity in trying former Nazis. Whether he
ordered the drugs that killed that particular infant, he was
certainly implicated in the killing project. He had
responsibility for the false records, and admitted filling out
many forms that resulted in children's deaths, and signing
large numbers of false death certificates. He is widely
suspected of having done much more: for a period of months
during his work at the institution when there was no head
doctor, children continued to die in ways considered
suspicious. To me he clearly sought to explain his
involvement in such a way as to minimize his responsibility.
But I believe he also conveyed accurately the deliberate
ambiguity that facilitated his actions and limited his sense
of guilt about whatever he did in connection with the killing.
This 'as if' situation is characteristic of direct medical killing
and, to a considerable extent, of indirect medicalized killing
as well.

F.'s youthful embrace of the Nazi movement in Bavaria
also had great bearing on his perceptions and actions. Having
been an unusually enthusiastic member of the Hitler Youth
and a Party member since he was eighteen, he was deeply
troubled by rumours he heard, while working in psychiatric
hospitals during the early 1940s, of the killing of the mentally
ill. He at first denounced these rumours as 'vicious
propaganda against the regime'; and when they could no
longer be denied, he still 'tried to see all of this somehow
in connection with the idealism of National Socialism.' He
had the need, that is, to seek, on the one hand, some
justification of the killing within the biomedical vision; and,
on the other hand, to continue to call forth defenses of denial
and psychic numbing, helped by the bureaucratic
medicalization of the program, in order to convince himself
that 'these forms [which he filled out] were absolutely

harmless,' and that even the policy of killing deformed children 'was not a command but a regulation giving the authorization so that the children *could* be killed.'

He described an interaction between the child-victim without ordinary human feelings ('whom one cannot speak to, who does not laugh, who is affectively unapproachable') and the physician-killer with the same malady ('Such an executioner does not have that bad feeling [that one has in directly killing a person] . . . There is a lack of the affective tension, the emotional participation . . . and that can turn any human being into a murderer').

Robert J. Lifton, *The Nazi Doctors*

This is why for several years, the French Medical Commission of Amnesty International has sought to encourage individual and collective consideration of 'the temptation of torture'. A questionnaire on the 'mini-violences' of medicine was sent out to several thousand doctors and nurses[10] and helped to identify some of the ambiguous situations: recalcitrant patients are tied up, bedridden patients force-fed, terminations of pregnancy carried out without anaesthetic, anorexics unlawfully locked up, sterilisations and abortions forcibly performed on gipsies and mental patients, medical examinations that are contrary to the interest of the patient, experiments done 'for commercial ends', and invasive examinations that are 'more useful to the medical faculty than the patient'. All these practices are regularly denounced by doctors and nurses for whom patients are entitled to respect. Many cases involve particular 'populations', meaning not only prisoners but also drug abusers, alcoholics, foreigners, marginals, old and handicapped people.[11] The majority of those who replied to the questionnaire saw the need to denounce these situations and to set respect for the patient above any notion of professional solidarity.

Compassion gone astray

Indicators of falling standards in general medicine, such as the dehumanisation of patients, bear a strange resemblance to the processes at work when doctors are involved in torture. Social misfits, handicapped or retarded people or those abandoned by their families are the first to be affected. To the clinical eye they can appear to be mere cases, or even 'less than cases', as Nurse Christiane Vollaire[12] explains: 'Health care staff find it hard to make contact with patients they regard almost as animals, such as people who are senile or dirty.' In psychiatric hospitals, the staff try to protect themselves against a feeling of destabilisation. Nurses are frequently instructed not to talk to the patients so as not to 'upset the psychiatrists' work'. The anonymity of the doctor-patient relationship, in fact a banal situation, was considered by the delegates at the 'Medicine at Risk' conference to be one of seven risk factors that can lead to torture in a prison. To a lesser degree, it also poses a problem in other institutions. The person who has arrived in the emergency department of a big city hospital at night in a 'coma due to alcohol overdose' has already become a number – just like a prisoner.

The patient is constantly at risk of ceasing to be a real person in the eyes of the doctor or the institution. This is partly because he is dependent, but also, as Professor Antoine Lazarus thinks, because of the same 'compassion gone astray' that plays a part in torture: 'The doctor can't bear to see the condition the patient is in and he feels powerless, so he doesn't care what he does, he treats the other person as an object. This is how people in the caring professions get hardened. In a way it's because they're too sensitive ... ' To Professor Tomkiewicz,[13] the same hardheartedness accounts for the use of 'aversive' behavioural methods in some American psychiatric hospitals: 'Psychotic children who mutilate themselves are an unbearable sight for the nursing staff. So in this context, it might seem justifiable to try to re-educate them with an electric "shepherd's crook". Later, this therapy will be extended to patients who are unbearable in more trivial ways: children who are messy eaters, for instance.'

Illness, particularly mental illness, can be unbearable to the observer, and this blocks the empathy that is essential to genuine compassion. In extreme contexts, such as that of

Nazi psychiatry, this reaction gave rise to a 'theory of lack of empathy',[14] a purely organic view of illness and its treatment, which opened the way to practising 'euthanasia' on 'incurables'. More commonly today, it can lead to a determination to apply treatment at all cost, sometimes without the patient's consent or at the price of bodily or spiritual violence. This is where we see the most highly technical medical developments, which are sometimes the most manipulative, being given preference at the expense of the relationship aspect of medical care. This category of treatment extends to behaviour modification, and new techniques of manipulating physiology, bio-rhythms, and the brain. This is where the sophisticated torturer will find that his tools of modern medicine support and justify. The inquisitorial and domineering character of torture is supported and justified by the investigative methods of modern medicine.

The end justifies the means

'Your moral standards have fallen,' says Professor Tomkiewicz, 'when you hear yourself saying that the end justifies the means.' The danger becomes acute when doctors come up against social, medical or prison institutions, and there is a clash with a higher interest. In a hospital or a medico-social establishment, the need to maintain discipline can push doctors towards constraint in treatment. A group of forensic specialists and psychiatrists explains:[15] 'When a doctor in an institution also has a managerial and disciplinary role, he may turn to the therapeutic arsenal at his disposal for the means of securing his power and authority.' Far from being at the patient's service, the use of neuroleptics, hydrotherapy and electric shocks then becomes a way of achieving peace and quiet. The isolation of the patient, and the fact that the establishment is relatively closed off from outside observation, add to the risk. Isolation is mental as well as physical. Clocks and watches are taken away in some psychiatric units as well as some prisons, and this contributes to the disorientation and dependence of the inmate. It certainly appears to be more of a punitive measure than a therapeutic one. The institutional framework lifts some of the responsibility from its employees, all the more so if the unit is restrictive and hierarchic.

The same problem can arise in the context of medico-legal and medico-social examinations, which seal the fate of prisoners (by judging their fitness for detention or isolation), defendants (by deciding on diminished or enhanced responsibility), or of handicapped people being sent to various types of more or less advanced homes or sheltered workshops. There is a risk that medical diagnosis may legitimise social policy, and be determined by technocratic or financial criteria. The concern to protect society, particularly in the case of psychiatry, can lead to hasty and definitive diagnoses which leave people profoundly marked. A man labelled pyromaniac at fifteen during a puberty crisis he will grow out of in a few years' time, can spend twenty years in a psychiatric hospital. Experimenting on people 'without a directly therapeutic aim' arises from the same process of forgetting the human subject in the name of a higher interest.

The greater and more constraining appears to be this higher interest, the more slippery is the slope towards a decline in ethical standards. Terrorism is supposed to justify torture and the death penalty, and the real or assumed danger posed by sick people also implies that therapeutic aims will be waived in favour of security aims. A prison doctor, or a hospital doctor on duty being asked questions by the police, will find it hard to insist on medical confidentiality in the patient's interest. The very principle of forensic medicine contradicts the guarantee of confidentiality. In a prison or military setting, or semi-custodial institutions such as 'special units for difficult patients', there is a permanent risk that the doctor or nurse will be 'a mere accessory in reducing the untimely manifestations' of the inmates.[16] A public health survey in France showed the extent to which 'the therapeutic aspect takes second place to the security aspect' in these special units.[17]

Regulation and resistance

Dehumanisation, the obliteration of the individual and his rights, the therapeutic relationship reduced to a technical gesture and the patient to a case, therapeutic objectives confused with disciplinary ones, the alleged superiority of scientific, socio-economic or political interests, and the lack of responsibility of medical staff in a hierarchic organisation: Here are thus some of the risk factors. Torture, its extreme refinement and its justification by medical personnel caught in a vicious spiral, stands at the extreme limit of declining ethical standards. Here, the higher interest becomes an overwhelmingly urgent reason of State, the victim is an enemy who must be destroyed, dependence is total, isolation implacable, and orders are without appeal. Torture presupposes an accumulation and exacerbation of these risk factors. But between the normal risk and this extreme risk, is there a difference of nature or only of degree?[18] In the following chapters we will analyse some of the intermediate situations which link the two extremes. We will see how medical ethics centred on the rights of the human being can help to prevent a major decline in ethical standards, by regulating forensic and prison medicine. The death penalty and judicial amputations, however, will emerge as legalised forms of torture, and therefore require a clear ethical decision in the form of a total refusal to take part. In all cases the only safeguard of professional ethics and weapon of resistance is the refusal to adopt a náive attitude and believe that all is for the best.

3 Forensic reports are never neutral

On 6 September 1977, the leader of the South African Black Consciousness Movement, Steve Biko, was arrested and taken to a police station for questioning. On 7 September at 7.30 a.m., Dr Ivor Lang, a doctor in the prison service, was called by the security police to examine Biko, whose behaviour, they told him, was 'odd'. Lang found several lesions on Biko's body. His movements were unco-ordinated and he was unable to speak. At the request of Colonel Goosen, the local chief of police, Dr Lang drafted a certificate stating: 'I found no abnormality and no pathological signs.' The next day, Lang examined Biko again, this time accompanied by his superior, Dr Benjamin Tucker. The patient was handcuffed to a grille, and lying on a rug soaked in urine. The doctors called in a private specialist, Dr Hersch, who performed a lumbar puncture. This revealed the presence of blood in the cerebrospinal fluid. Yet the doctors raised no objection to Biko's being kept in detention. On 11 September, Biko was found unconscious. Dr Tucker suggested taking him to hospital, but Colonel Goosen refused. Dr Tucker then agreed to Biko's being taken by car to Pretoria, about 750 miles away. He died during the night of the 12th, without medical assistance.

In July 1985, Dr Lang was still the district surgeon in Port Elizabeth. On his instructions, Dr Wendy Orr examined a number of people arrested under the State of Emergency. But she broke the silence. In a sworn affidavit to the Supreme Court in September 1985, she stated that a great many of her patients told her they had been tortured, and presented marks that bore out their allegations. She added that she had already informed the authorities. With the support of church representation, she asked the Court to take appropriate action. The Court passed a temporary injunction preventing policemen from ill-treating detainees. Most of the people Wendy Orr had examined were released at the end of 1985, and her action served to draw international attention to the ill-treatment suffered by prisoners in South Africa. Wendy Orr's superiors in the hierarchy did not forgive her. She was transferred to a geriatric unit, and then, threatened by anonymous letters, decided to leave the area at the end of 1985.

'Evaluate' or condone

One country's system of medical reporting led to two diametrically opposite results. One expert condoned torture, another denounced it. In the first case, a man died; in the second, prisoners were protected and freed.

'It is a contravention of medical ethics for health personnel, particularly physicians, to be involved in any professional relationship with prisoners or detainees the purpose of which is not solely to evaluate, protect or improve their physical and mental health,' says Principle 3 of the UN Principles of Medical Ethics. The word 'evaluate' is important here, as Amnesty International Legal Adviser Nigel Rodley stresses. If evaluation is always directed towards the protection or recovery of the patient, there should be no need to mention it explicitly. Conversely, there can be no ethically acceptable form of medical evaluation other than that which aims to protect and treat the patient. Can evaluation be neutral and objective with respect to the patient's interests?

During his trial, Dr Lang was cross-examined by Sydney Kentridge, the Biko family's lawyer. 'Does the Hippocratic Oath not bind you to set the interest of your patient above any other consideration? In this affair, did you subordinate that interest to security considerations?' – 'Yes,' Lang replied, to both questions. The doctor's evaluative function, whether it be in the form of a simple oral diagnosis or of an official certificate, cannot be neutral. If the doctor in question neglects the interest of the patient and is subject to pressure for other purposes from a higher authority, there is a risk that the doctor will lose sight of his ethical obligations and do no more than approve the acts of the higher authority. 'Although it is rare to see doctors actually carrying out the task of the hangman, they fulfil a much more important medical function, which is that of legitimising the use of torture or any suffering inflicted on a human body,' say Dr Lenoir *et al.*[1] 'The doctor allows the executive agent to act without guilt, since his action will fall within a zone demarcated by medical and scientific reference.'

The question is not so much whether the evaluation is truthful, as whether it has been deliberately separated from all therapeutic intention, or from any help given to the patient. 'The word "evaluate",' Nigel Rodley explains, 'is important. One of the important roles that is often given to doctors, particularly with regard to capital punishment, is indeed the obligation to certify fitness for the execution.' Here again, medical expertise is trapped by a higher interest, although it is provided in good faith. By agreeing to answer the question, 'Is this man fit to be executed?', the examining doctor is not being dishonest in the same way as a doctor who signs a false certificate. He is, however, betraying his vocation, by condoning an act which, by definition, runs counter to the patient's health. He is being dishonest in giving the impression that such 'fitness for execution' could have any meaning in a medical or scientific sense. As Nigel Rodley says, 'Exactly what medical criteria can be used to decide whether somebody is fit to be killed, or fit to be maimed, has always eluded me. Presumably doctors are being asked to certify something medical in a concept which is inherently anti-medical.'

'What can "fitness for detention" or "fitness for isolation" mean?' Dr Gonin and Dr Buffard wonder.[2] 'Is there also such a thing as fitness for torture or the death penalty?' The doctor 'perceives to the full the detrimental consequences of detention on prisoners' physical and mental health, and it is he who is asked to certify as true something that can never be true, namely that such-and-such a person is fit to be detained ... Delinquents are often complacently described as maladjusted, deficient, anti-social and violent, but to declare them fit for a life of reclusion devoid of all stimulation and responsibility, and deprived of personal relationships, would constitute a paradox in any rational system.'

One extreme result of this paradox is the systematic solitary confinement of South African prisoners: 'prisoners who have been in solitary confinement for a considerable length of time and have symptoms of solitary confinement such as depersonalisation, depression, traumatic stress disorder, etc, are eventually declared fit by psychiatrists in State hospitals to go back into solitary confinement again' says a member of NAMDA,[3] the anti-apartheid medical association which was set up in the wake of the Biko affair. At the other extreme, compulsory daily medical examination of prisoners in solitary confinement ('the cooler') in ordinary prisons, and the doctor's power to suspend that punishment on medical grounds, often constitute a guarantee against the possible deterioration of the prisoner's health. In both cases, neutrality stops at the point where the prisoner starts to suffer, and where a doctor's decision can either prolong and condone that suffering, or 'set the interest of the patient above any other consideration'.

Here again international standards do not help clarify matters. The UN 'Standard Minimum Rules for the Treatment of Prisoners, implicitly authorising prison punishments such as isolation and deprivation of food, require that a doctor should supervise their application. This could be either protection of the prisoner or condonement of the system. The British Medical Association has clarified the rules by deciding: 'If any diet is so restrictive that medical monitoring is necessary, that diet is inhumane, and no doctor should be associated with it.'

'Doctor Death'

A psychiatric examination of an accused prior to the passing of a sentence or committal to a mental institution may also influence the verdict, whether this be to declare the accused unfit for any form of punishment or fit only for a certain type of punishment. The role of doctors in the death penalty in the USA is an extreme example.

This man would be socially maladjusted in the extreme. Nothing can be done for him from a medical or a psychiatric point of view, or even as regards any reinsertion in society. His behaviour will not change wherever he is. . .

Dr James P. Grigson, a Dallas psychiatrist and expert witness to the courts, has made this type of prediction his speciality. In the past eighteen years he has been a witness in 111 trials, of which 102 ended in death sentences. His signature gives psychiatric justification to the death penalty by designating a category of defendants who cannot be rehabilitated. His evaluations are now being contested by the American Psychiatric Association. 'Psychiatrists have not demonstrated their ability to make long-term predictions of violent behaviour,' says Dr Paul Appelbaum of the APA. But despite a major press campaign, the Dallas District Attorney still calls on Dr Grigson's advice. '"Doctor Death" will still do his worst. . .'[4]

The criminal justice system in many countries expects a psychiatric witness to pronounce on the state of mind of the accused at the time of the facts, and also on his eligibility for punishment. This rests on the logic of applying labels to people, which often is tantamount to a condemnation. In France, the use of Article 64 of the Criminal Code, despite its protective aspects, has been raising questions among psychiatrists and jurists for many years. 'To deny the imputability of the facts is also to deny the perpetrator of the facts as an individual,' in the view of some psychiatrists,[5] 'and to deprive him of a trial which might prove him innocent.' 'How could the expert witness fail to indulge in intellectual contortions to explain that the accused was or was not in a state of insanity at the time of the acts which may not have been committed by him, while at the same time specifying whether or not there is anything disquieting about his personality?' a French judge wrote recently in *Le Monde*.[6] 'The importance of the psychiatric expert in criminal proceedings has increased considerably in recent years. Only very exceptionally is it a question of knowing whether the accused was in a state of insanity at the time of the event; the psychiatrist is expected to throw light on the mental functioning of the accused.'

Dr Claude Aigues-Vives, a Nîmes psychiatrist and member of the Amnesty International Medical Commission, explains that this appraisal can have far-reaching consequences:

> They're demanding a clear-cut answer to an unclear problem.
> So the psychiatrist turns a spotlight on this or that aspect of the
> person, emphasises a 'perverse tendency', and signs a warrant
> for a long sentence or, on the contrary, puts the stress on an
> unhappy childhood, which will be tantamount to a mitigating
> circumstance. What juries don't know is that you can't sum up
> all the aspects of a human person in a single word. But that
> one word might prove fatal.

The normal and the pathological

Lies, truth or half-truth? The question is already crucial when
there is a risk that an expert's opinion may implant the idea
of guilt in the minds of a jury, although proof of guilt requires
completely different methods. The risk becomes acute when
a psychiatrist's diagnosis of danger to society is the sole ground
for sending someone to prison or a mental institution.

'Schizokomystia' ('schizo-divergence of opinion'), 'recon-
struction-of-society mania', and 'asymptomatic psychosis' are
some of the categories Soviet psychiatrists created in the 1970s
to assimilate nonconformity or political dissent into a framework of mental illness. This shows the extent to which the
psychiatric profession as a whole had become a vassal of the
Party and the State, which all Soviet doctors are pledged to
serve. But even here, matters are not clear-cut. 'Interpreting
behaviour is extremely difficult,' says Dr Jean-Luc Nahel, who
co-ordinated psychiatric missions to the Eastern bloc in 1988
for 'Médecins sans Frontières'.

> Some psychiatrists came back saying 'We saw people being perse-
> cuted.' Others said, 'We saw some really sick people who weren't
> getting the treatment they needed.' In some cases they were talk-
> ing about the same people ... Behaviour described in the French
> medical nosography as 'passionate idealism' may in some contexts
> be considered pathological, while in others it would be justified
> by the environmental structure.

'Apart from the fact that people are put into hospital when
they show no signs whatsoever of psychiatric disorder,'
says Dr Dominique Martin,[7] 'there are also mentally-ill

patients, or those suffering from relatively mild neurosis, languishing in a very crude system where everyone is labelled schizophrenic' – especially if they disturb the social order. But even in the Western world, where psychiatric nosography is more influenced by psychoanalytical theories than by the Pavlovian mechanism, and seems less tied to social norms, the motives for 'automatic confinement' are sometimes staggering. A smallholder who objects to the reallocation of her land, or a civil servant with no previous history of mental illness who suddenly finds he has been classed as schizophrenic and sent to hospital after psychological tests, are all too often the kind of people who bear the brunt of simplistic diagnosis.

It is not always clear whether this diagnosis will help or harm the patient. A diagnosis of 'normality', i.e. of fitness for punishment, might condemn a defendant to prison, and elsewhere to the gulag or death, rather than to a 'milder' punitive committal to a mental hospital. But the fate of inmates in Soviet or Romanian psychiatric hospitals is far from enviable. And, as Dr Robert Kirschner[8] explains:

> While under exceptional circumstances I think it's beneficial for the psychiatrist to issue certificates to protect the person, I think there's a danger inherent in this in always creating a medical model for unpopular behaviour, because in a sense it tends to reinforce the authorities who may think that any form of 'deviant behaviour' is in fact a manifestation of a mental disease or disorder.

Confessions

Whether it is to assess the condition of the person or of his very personality, the game of medical truth is not to be played with impunity. An examining doctor cannot disregard society's need to be protected against delinquency and crime, nor the possibility that the accused may be dangerous. But conversely, the use of a psychiatric evaluation in prosecution evidence does resemble, with all due reserves, the central role given to confessions by the British anti-terrorist courts when establishing a person's guilt. In both cases, the accused has to be 'made to talk'. This involves the risk of embarking on an inquisitorial procedure, coupled with a breach of trust. 'The good doctor, as an expert witness becomes a witness for the prosecution, and is released from professional confidentiality. The accused does not always realise this, and he will talk to the doctor in confidence, when the doctor hasn't explained what is at stake in the interview,' says Professor Lazarus. Conversely, if the patient is suspicious, Dr Claude Aigues-Vives says, the doctor 'will find it hard to cope with the stubborn silence, and will try to latch on to things in the little he already knows, and risk causing the accused to break down'. To a much lesser degree, this is the same process as torture, where 'making someone talk' and finding out 'the Truth' has no therapeutic connotations, unless confession can be considered a form of treatment. The caricature of this determination to get at the truth about a person, beyond the appearances that are obvious to the layman, comes out in the systematic suspicion in the Eastern bloc that nonconformists are 'covering up' the mental illness they are supposed to have. The psychiatrist is also in an ambiguous position in a prison context, where he is associated with the choice of conditions of detention, hospitalisation or other forms of treatment for the prisoner. 'The doctor takes part in working out the strategy by which the guilty person is expected to mend his ways, but also to pay the penalty for his crime', say the three authors quoted above.[9] So there is a risk that the psychiatrist will expect the prisoner to show 'repentance', recognition that he has done wrong, and remorse. If necessary, he will force along the process of self-examination by giving psychotherapy. So evaluation becomes inquisition, and a psychiatric cure leads to recantation.

The ultimate stage in such a violation of the patient's privacy is the way torturers make use of information about the victim's personality. In Uruguay, according to Dr Francisco Ottonelli,[10]

> notes about the prisoners' clinical examinations have been passed on to the military, who have then used them in planning torture. This means that medical material which ought to have been used solely for the good of the patient has been used by the military

to identify the victim's weak points ... It is very important to preserve medical secrecy so that information about the prisoner should be used only to protect his health.

The same problem arises with the instruction to South African nurses to report to the district medical officer, police station or army, if they suspect their patients of terrorist activities, or again in this advice given by a Danish doctor during a police interrogation: 'If you want him to talk, go ahead now. He's very tired.' In all these cases, to varying degrees, the precise intimate knowledge of the person and his condition which is granted by clinical access, is deflected away from its therapeutic purpose.

Responsible evaluation

Does then any examination or assessment of the physical or mental state of persons in repressive surroundings constitute a trap? The experience of the French Medical Commission of Amnesty International, of treatment centres for torture victims, forensic specialists and prison doctors shows the contrary to be the case. Secrecy is not an end in itself, and can be deleterious if its aim is not to protect the patient, but to protect the authorities against public opinion. A medical report can be a way of protecting the patient or supporting reparation, provided that this objective is kept in mind and counterbalances the interests of superior forces, of the State or society. Such a reversal of logic will require, however, a great degree of independence, courage and lucidity on the part of doctors caught in a conflict of interests. Dr Wendy Orr, by refusing to keep evidence of ill-treatment to herself, restored the protective role of the medical report. If autopsies were carried out as a matter of course, by an independent doctor, they would act as a deterrent to the ill-treatment of prisoners. The despatch of independent experts (see box on p. 34), the training of doctors to recognise traces of violence, the giving of power to prison doctors to withdraw a sick

prisoner, after diagnosis, from harmful living conditions open
up possibilities for improvement.

Second opinion in El Salvador

In May 1988, two young men had been shot, at least that
was the allegation; they were tortured and shot by the military
in a deserted area in the north-east of El Salvador. They had
been buried for three months and there was a court order
that they could be exhumed and autopsied. I was asked by
AAAS to go to El Salvador to do the exhumation on that
particular day. So I went there. The authorities didn't know
I was coming, and they did have a local forensic pathologist
paid by the Americans. He was there, and he was there on
the spot, and he didn't like my presence. He had a very bad
reputation in the population. This man was a doctor at risk.
Some of these doctors are doctors at risk because they want
to, because of fear of repression, of the government, of the
loss of income, the loss of their life, or whatever. So he let
me do all the work under the burning sun and as soon as
I had the two bodies on the ground, he would step in and
try to obstruct my work. Each time I turned my back, on
him, on the bodies, he would take some pieces and make
my work worse. But this guy, he also knew that when I came
home I would write a report, and he knew that if I wrote
a report to, say, an American magazine, an American medical
journal, he would be exposed as being one of the tools for
the government, one of the repressors, like he had been a
lot of times before, but without any foreign specialist or
people coming in trying to control what he was doing, or what
was happening. This was the first time. So I wrote my report
and at the same time he wrote his report, stating that in his
mind there was no doubt that these people had been killed
by the military. I'm sure he had had contact with the military,
and they had arranged this, because the colonel from that
particular brigade had admitted that something happened out
there, his soldiers were involved, he would give no names,
but it means they admitted what was happening. And this
in my opinion is the kind of support and education and
information we can give to foreign countries, also of course
in our own country if that's possible. You can have fear to
suffer, that you or your family will suffer, but you can also

have fear to be exposed, and this is the essence of education
and information.

> Dr Jorgen Thomsen, member of the Committee of Concerned
> Forensic Scientists, Denmark; presentation to the
> 'Medicine at Risk' conference

However, a certain number of rules have to be observed.
'The doctor will establish a more ethical relationship with
the accused if he does not conceal the purpose of the medical
examination,' says Professor Lazarus. The Declaration of
Hawaii[11] states moreover: 'If and when a relationship is established for purposes other than therapeutic, such as in forensic
psychiatry, its nature must be thoroughly explained to the
person concerned.' In Dr Aigues-Vives's view, the priority
is to 'refrain from a method of interrogation that might risk
making the accused break down, or from entering into a therapeutic relationship which the examining doctor is not there
to establish', and also to weigh up the conclusions about the
accused. The right to a second opinion should serve to coun-
teract the one-sided nature of some diagnoses. There is therefore a possibility of establishing a code of ethics for forensic
examinations and reports, which would be less categorical
or 'invasive'. Treatment centres for torture victims, and doctors who help them provide proof of ill-treatment, have shown
that it is possible to find out the truth without endangering
people through a desperate desire to know.

Independence and responsibility are the main criteria of
this code of ethics. This is far removed from the 'mirage'
of neutrality. As Dr Said Sadi has said,[12] 'In the medical
expert's task there is room to "adopt a position".' Just as
a medical examination or report may represent an approval,
so a prison visit which is too 'neutral' may be transformed
into an alibi. Neutrality evades responsibility. This is also
true of the contents of the medical report. 'The psychiatrist
and the doctor should beware of claims to "objectivity",' says
Dr Lamothe.[13] 'They should recognise that they are subjec-
tive, and simply involved, as in most medical actions, in the
unavoidable drama of deciding what is best for someone else.'

4 Prison doctors and hunger strikes

Despite their claims to neutrality and objectivity, doctors responsible for official medical examinations and reports are thus in a risk situation. Once again, the involvement of doctors in torture and executions, thereby putting their seal of approval on these practices, prompts us to investigate the question of risk indicators, in order to combat the sometimes fatal deterioration in ethical standards which can result from the 'naïveté' of doctors. In view of 'the gradual erosion of the ethical rules' (Dr John Dawson[1]), several working groups at the 'Medicine at Risk' conference devoted a great deal of time to discussing the circumstances which precede torture.

In discussing risk indicators particular attention was given to one place, prison, and to one situation, a detainee's hunger strike. As to the former, Dr Léry points out that 'all closed places are areas of risk', prison is their archetype and the place where tensions run highest, since it is explicitly designed to punish, and is a direct expression of the power of the State. As to the hunger strike, it not only puts the prisoner's life at risk but also challenges the classic principles of medical ethics, which are based on the preservation of life. Dr Espinoza, the doctor in charge of Fresnes Prison Hospital, describes the position of a prison doctor during a hunger strike as 'between the Devil and the deep blue sea'.

Prisoners condemned to ill-health?

The prison population, from the outset, is not a healthy one, and the prison system in itself gives rise to a whole range of pathological cases. 'Doctors, and all health staff, are in an ambiguous position in prison,' say four doctors from Lyons.[2] 'They are the guarantors of the right to health, or rather the right to treatment, which in principle is not altered by the fact of detention. But the treatment is given to people whose conditions of existence are incompatible with the maintenance of physical and mental equilibrium.' Under the title 'Are prisoners condemned to ill-health?', in June 1988 the medical journal *Tonus* published a fairly damning account of the health conditions in French prisons, which are by no means exceptionally bad.[3]

> When the courts pass a sentence of imprisonment, they do not at the same time sentence the prisoner to be deprived of medical treatment. But woe betide the convict who also happens to be diabetic, or a drug addict, or suffering from TB or Aids or a stomach ulcer. Months or years in prison won't mean the same thing to him as they would to a young man or a professional criminal in good health. More often than not he will have to do battle with the prison authorities to get a doctor's visit, or a special diet, or essential drugs for his condition, or to get admitted to a civilian hospital. One hour's attendance per prisoner per year to deal with the systematic examination of new arrivals, care of the sick, responding to emergencies, treatment of drug addicts and Aids cases, general hygiene, health care for the prison staff, filling in numerous certificates, forms and case records, and writing up reports – this is the incredible feat accomplished every day by the hundreds of general practitioners who have contracted to do a specific term of prison work.

One of the recommendations of the 'Medicine at Risk' conference was:

> If there is a difference in the standard of care or access to care within prison and outside prison, that would be an indicator that the potential for the abuse of human rights existed. So the quality of care in prison and access to that care should be the same inside the prison population as it is for any population outside the prison.

This may seem to be aiming high, but it simply recapitulates the first principle of medical ethics as defined by the United Nations. It also reflects the experience of doctors who have lived under dictatorship, particularly in Uruguay. Forensic specialists in Montevideo[4] describe cases of prison medical practice which should not be tolerated, including 'omission, negligence or incompetence on the part of medical staff', 'non-existent or infrequent clinical examinations; the same drug uniformly prescribed for all patients with the same disorder', and also a lack of 'follow-up examinations of illnesses that are only treated symptomatically'. Similarly, the Medical Association of South Africa, MASA,[5] asked in a report in May 1982 for every prisoner to have the right to consult the doctor of his own choice. Should we consider such demands as luxuries or, on the contrary, as solid guarantees against abuses?

Strict prison regimes can be exacerbated by an exceptional political situation (the beginning of a dictatorship, or civil war), or by a political structure (apartheid) or by a conflict within the prison (mutiny, hunger strike, or ill-treatment by a guard or fellow-prisoner). In such cases, mere negligence can have fatal consequences. There was a tragic example of this in the Uruguayan military hospital where Gladys Yanes, Miguel Coitino and many others died in the early 1980s without adequate medical care. Angel Maria Yoldi Aricet died of cancer after a single unrepeated course of chemotherapy. 'I saw some incredible things in there,' writes a former prisoner. 'Selva Braselli had an ear infection that wouldn't get better, but she was refused antibiotics. They took x-rays of her uninfected ear, to prove to the Red Cross that everything was all right.' Five months went by before Selva Braselli saw a specialist, then another four weeks between the taking of the ear swab and the arrival of the prescription. In August 1984, a third of the 523 political prisoners in Uruguay were ill. All of them had been tortured, and were being held in an atmosphere of extreme insecurity and tension.

In South Korea, thirty-five prisoners on hunger strike announced on 30 January 1989 that prisoners had died without receiving medical attention. In Turkey, ten prisoners who were beaten while being transferred to isolation cells in May 1989 were not taken to hospital, despite having broken ribs and nose fractures. Every week, Amnesty International's 'urgent medicalactions' reveal cases of death through indifference. In the Archambault top-security prison in Canada, after a riot in 1982, an Amnesty delegation, which included a doctor, concluded that there had been culpable negligence on the part of the health staff. A prisoner who had probably been beaten up after the riot was thought to be a malingerer, and was given nothing but aspirin for several months. A woman lawyer, alerted by another prisoner, saw at once that Jason Gallant, who was vomiting a foul-smelling fluid, probably had an intestinal obstruction in an advanced stage due to his alleged ill-treatment. A general lack of concern for the inmates' state of health in this very tough prison, combined with fear on the part of the health staff, a fear exacerbated by violent incidents, had almost resulted in an irreversible loss of medical ethics.

Closer to us, a French prisoner filed an official complaint in 1988 after having spent five days without medical treatment and then having been transported from northern France to Fresnes hospital, when he had a ruptured spleen from being beaten up by fellow-prisoners. These violations of the right to health do not in themselves amount to maltreatment, but they create a climate in which a deterioration of the physical or mental condition of a prisoner is more easily accepted. Dr Benasayag describes how surprising and 'ironic' it was to come out of prison after four years and suddenly see so much attention, equipment and medical care put at the service of his health. 'It just seemed so very strange ... that they were taking so much trouble to protect my life. It was odd that the idea of dying could be taken seriously, and that it could be unimaginable for anyone ill not to have immediate care and drugs at his disposal.'[6] Even if the average prison does not have a great deal in common with the torturing harshness and torture prevailing in Argentinian military prisons, many prisoners would be entitled to share this sense of irony. When situations of extra restrictions or violence arise, seeping contempt for the individual and his body will provide just the conditions for a decline in ethical standards. Conflicts or violent episodes in a prison will bring about a reciprocal decline in health standards.

From care to constraint

The other side of prison medicine is the use of treatment as part of the logic of constraint, the use of the prescription

in a system of alternate favours and punishments which per-
verts its effect. Here again, extreme examples can be found
in situations of dictatorship or conflict. In the so-called 'Libertad' prison in Uruguay, according to former detainees, Dr
Britos, a psychologist, master-minded during ten years a
scientific policy of destabilisation of prisoners. He would
have contributed to the development of a particularly subtle
and perverse system of capricious decisions and interference
with prisoners' normal points of reference:[7] discrimination
between the different floors of the prison without apparent
reason, constant changes and transfers, and spells in solitary
confinement. Medical care was part of the system: seeing a
doctor or going to hospital was a favour, handed out arbi-
trarily. It was also a punishment: a prisoner could be taken
to hospital, even in a coma, with his hands tied, in an army
vehicle, after standing and waiting for five hours. In hospital,
the patients were not allowed to talk or read or do handicrafts.
The women were frequently insulted and strip-searched. Massive doses of tranquillisers were used to keep order and to
disorientate the prisoners still further, while neuroleptics, used
without medication to control side-effects, became veritable
instruments of torture (see Chapter 6). In Argentina, particularly cruel 'methods' of delivering babies[8] employed by Dr
Bergès represented another example of punitive 'treatment'.

But here again, ethical standards had deteriorated before
the abuses took place. The Montevideo forensic specialists,
and the delegates at the 'Medicine at Risk' conference, identified several indicators of declining standards: medical experiments,   medical   intervention   without   anaesthetic,
punishment for refusing to take a drug, treatment being given
under conditions set by the administration, and bartering
medical treatment in exchange for co-operation.

In Uruguay, Dr Ottonelli says, 'doctors accused of failing
in their professional duty defended themselves by saying they
weren't responsible for applying the treatment'. Gloria Lab-
lanca is a doctor who was imprisoned in Punta de Rieles from
1972 to 1982. When she talks about the arbitrary way drugs
were distributed – digestive remedies taken on an empty
stomach, sleeping pills three hours before bedtime – she

unwittingly holds up a curious mirror to the practice of ordinary prison medicine. 'The prescription will be adopted into the prison ritual,' says Dr Maltaverne.[9] In some cases, psychotropic drugs are looked forward to, and initially prescribed, as a means of escape. If they are then administered under the eye of a warder at 7 p.m. or even 5 p.m., the prisoner loses the benefit of a period of calm when he could have regained his balance, and the drugs become a 'prison within a prison'. In other cases, readily-available drugs are directly prescribed by the warders. It is never possible to refuse to take medicines.

> The prisoner's health does not belong to him ... he can't chose his doctor or his medicines. He can't even refuse, and take responsibility for his own refusal. That ultimate possibility is taken over by the prison ritual, which turns a voluntary refusal into deprivation and punishment: if you refuse to take your medicine, it's withdrawn until the doctor grants the privilege again.

Similarly, a prisoner may be persuaded to take part in a medical experiment in exchange for a remission of sentence or an improvement in conditions; or a course of treatment outside the prison may be bartered for information given to the authorities. These practices are a perversion of medical treatment.

Another step towards a deterioration in professional ethics occurs when doctors take part in measures that have more to do with keeping order than providing medical care. A flagrant example is the involvement of prison medical staff in body-searches in many countries, including the United States. The choice is less clear when a doctor is asked to help 'restrain' an 'agitated' patient, or give him an injection of tranquillisers. In France, it is a legal requirement for a doctor to be present in this situation. In fact, as Dr Bernard Jomier[10] says,

> The doctor is generally faced with a *fait accompli*. Should he trust the prisoner, and untie him? What if he attacks a guard? How can he get out of this situation without approving a coercive method, or appearing to be a tool of the authorities, or misjudging how dangerous the prisoner might be?[11]

Should he give the injection that the warders demand? The problem is indeed complex: on the one hand, the presence of a doctor in these circumstances is a guarantee for the prisoner which is not available in many countries, and it would be dangerous to go back on it. On the other hand, there is a great danger of the doctor's becoming a medical arm for the maintenance of order in the prison, since the prescription of a neuroleptic does not always have a therapeutic function. Fear will be a factor in the deterioration of the doctor–patient relationship, as it is in old people's homes and mental homes. 'If the doctor lets fear get the upper hand, he will reduce the patient to an object,' Professor Antoine Lazarus says. 'A prison doctor will have to be very strong to gain the respect of the inmates and the administration.' Fear is the justification for warders' being present during a medical consultation, which is another risk indicator for prison doctors. Once more the question has to be asked: whom should the doctor be serving – the patient or the authorities? The non-existence of confidentiality in prisons shows the difficulty in promoting an independent medicine 'between the Devil and the deep blue sea'. Although it is hard to establish a good doctor–patient relationship in a prison context, the quality of that relationship is the best guarantee that ethical standards will be maintained.

The hunger strike dilemma

When a prison doctor is faced with 'auto-aggressive' behaviour, such as self-mutilation, attempted suicide, or hunger strikes, all of which are very common in prison, his dilemma becomes more dramatic. Violence to his own body is often the prisoner's only way of making people listen to him. A prisoner may swallow hundreds of needles to obtain a pass. 'It isn't just auto-aggression,' says Dr Jomier, 'it's a way of asserting his own existence and testing his strength against the prison authorities.' A hunger strike is a major transgression of medical ethics and also of the legal basis of States subject to the rule of law, which proclaim respect for the integrity of the human body and human life.[12] By putting his health and his life in the balance, the prisoner aims to make society responsible for this perversion: he does not wish to die, but he feels death would be preferable to the fate to which he has been condemned. In many cases, the administration will be prepared to go to any lengths to avoid giving in, and medical techniques for force-feeding can help it to do so. How can the doctor, without disclaiming his responsibility in the outcome of the conflict, which may be fatal, avoid acting as the mere technical arm of the authorities?

The clinical and biological criteria for judging the risk to the hunger striker are not clearly defined. There is a general consensus in favour of postponing admission to hospital for the first ten days, which are a period of adaptation, characterised by a deterioration in his general condition (500 grams of weight loss per day), a drop in blood pressure, and abdominal pains. Complications rarely occur before the twentieth day. These may be oedemas, myocardial impairment, and multiple neurological disorders, and they entail a risk of irreversible after-effects, and indeed of death. Eventually it will be necessary to make a prognosis of survival, and the question of force-feeding by naso-gastric tube or intravenously will arise. In France, only a doctor is authorised – but not bound by law[13] – to take that decision, but he will be put under considerable pressure, which will increase in proportion to the prisoner's fame and the amount of media coverage (see box).

> Should he be saved against his will, in defiance of his liberty and dignity? Should the doctor unreservedly become an ally in a suicidal battle, at the risk of laying himself open to a criminal charge? Should he sit by and watch the prisoner's slow death, and then step in and resuscitate the patient when he finally loses consciousness? ... The vocation to save life, apart from the fact that it remains fundamentally bound to the practice of medicine, may be considered an aggravating circumstance in a failure to help a person in danger.[14]

Mr Ben Bella's refusal

In November 1961, nearly four thousand Algerians in French prisons went on a hunger strike, which caused a great deal

of international concern, in order to gain recognition as
political prisoners. Their leaders, Mr Ben Bella and ministers
of the GPRA (Provisional Government of the Republic of
Algeria) were held initially in the Château de Turquant, and
then transferred on 14 November to the Raymond-Poincaré
Hospital in Garches, on the thirteenth day of a strict water-
only diet.

At the request of General de Gaulle and Mr Bernard
Chenot, the Minister of Justice, a delegation of doctors led by
Professor de Vernejoul, President of the Medical Council, and
Professor Hamburger, went to visit Mr Ben Bella and two of
his companions (Mr Aït-Ahmed and Mr Mohammed Khidder).

Professor de Vernejoul was kind enough to give us an
account of this interview (see below).

Following pressing interventions from the Moroccan
government, the United Nations General Assembly, and
above all the International Red Cross (Mr Boissier, from
Geneva, intervened personally after a visit to the detention
centre), the hunger strikes were stopped after twenty days.
The prisoners had not accepted any medical help, and
consequently none was imposed on them.

At the beginning of 1962, I was called in by the Minister
of Justice (who was then Mr Bernard Chenot), in my
capacity as President of the French Medical Association.
The Minister informed me of General de Gaulle's earnest
wish to put an end to Mr Ben Bella's hunger strike, as his
state of health was beginning to cause anxiety.

It was therefore decided to appoint a committee,
consisting of Professor Hamburger who was entrusted with
supervising the hunger striker's health, and Professors René
Moreau, Georges Boudin, and Albert Sarrazin. I myself
was asked to go and see Mr Ben Bella and persuade him
not to continue with a strike which could endanger his life.
I accepted the mission, and went to see Mr Ben Bella, who
was being held under house arrest in the Paris suburbs.
I was accompanied by Mr Schmelk, who was then the
Director of Prison Administration and is now the senior
judge at the Supreme Court of Appeal. We had our first
interview with Mr Ben Bella, who was lying down and very
emaciated, looking tired and stern, but perfectly in control
of himself and most polite.

I explained the mission the government had entrusted

me with, and added that in my capacity as a doctor I could have no other aim than to protect his life and to ensure that his decision to take no food should not become a danger to that life. In view of these facts, I asked him if he would temper the severity of the hunger strike, and accept, for example, that what he drank should be something other than plain water.

I met with an absolute refusal.

This man proved to have an indomitable will. I was sitting beside him, and put my hand on his arm in a mechanical gesture. He thought I was about to take his pulse, and pushed me away roughly, saying 'No, Professor, don't try to examine me. I won't accept that, from you or anyone.'

I moved further away, and as I was achieving nothing, I finally asked: 'Mr Ben Bella, what would you do if we took the decision to feed you against your will?'

His expression became hard and stern. He looked me straight in the eye and said, 'If you did that, Professor, I would forever withdraw my respect for you and for all French doctors. Moreover I must warn you that you would never achieve your aims unless you put me to sleep.'

I recovered myself, and said, 'Please keep calm, Mr Ben Bella. No doctor, myself least of all, could allow himself to use force or an anaesthetic on you against your will.'

There remained nothing more for us to do than to report to the Minister of Justice on the total failure of our mission.

Days went by, and Mr Ben Bella's condition steadily deteriorated. I was then asked to have another interview with him, to ask if he would allow a blood sample to be taken, so as to judge the seriousness of his condition.

There was another absolute refusal. I had failed again. And when I tried my best to make him understand that his life was in danger, he always gave the same reply: 'Only the government can take the measures that would enable me to start eating.'

I reported back on this iron will that no doctor would be able to bend.

Professor Robert de Vernejoul, former President of the Ordre National des Médecins (French Medical Association), in *Le Monde*, 20 May 1981

In fact, if Article 63 of the French penal code concerning 'failure to help a person in danger', or its Danish or Belgian equivalent, is rarely invoked in cases of this kind, this is because Western medical practice rests on a 'contractual' concept of the doctor–patient relationship, which has been in force in France since 1936. This means that therapeutic treatment is given under a genuine contract, based on giving the patient full information about his state of health, the risks involved, the different forms of treatment to be considered, and their respective advantages and drawbacks. Referring to this concept, a judgment by the Supreme Court of Appeal makes the logical deduction that 'The offence of failure to help a person in danger may not be upheld against a doctor who ordered an adequate therapy which was not applied due to an obstinate and aggressive refusal by the patient.'

The same notion of a contract forms the basis of the recommendations on ethics and conduct in the Tokyo Declaration:

> When a prisoner refuses nourishment and is considered by the doctor as capable of forming an unimpaired and rational judgment concerning the consequences of such a voluntary refusal of nourishment, he or she shall not be fed artificially. The decision as to the capacity of the prisoner to form such a judgment should be confirmed by at least one other independent doctor. The consequences of the refusal of nourishment shall be explained by the doctor to the prisoner.

This approach, which may appear to contradict the doctor's obligation to protect life, is not unanimously supported. It was overruled in France in 1980, when Corsican separatists were intravenously force-fed, despite the opposition of Dr Forget, who was the senior doctor at Fresnes Prison at the time. In Israeli prisons, force-feeding is systematic. Dr Cohen Hadad, the senior doctor in the Israeli prison service, explained his reasons to the World Congress on Prison Medicine:

> There is no such thing as a hunger strike. There is just a prisoner who refuses to eat. Any prisoner who falls into that category is put under continuous medical surveillance. When his health

begins to deteriorate, generally from the fifth day onwards, the prisoner is fed by mouth if he consents. If he refuses, he is fed by naso-gastric tube, and in certain cases, intravenously.

He concluded by saying that he and his colleagues 'succeeded by these means in feeding four hundred prisoners for forty-five days, without any serious complications'.[15]

Such firmness sometimes has dramatic consequences. In Morocco, young people, arrested in January 1984 during demonstrations against high prices, began rotating hunger strikes to obtain adequate conditions of detention and medical care. On 23 June 1984, when their demands were refused, eight of them started an open-ended hunger strike. Two died in August of the same year. After Professor Minkovski[16] intervened, the other six, who had by then gone into a coma, were resuscitated in Averroes Hospital in Casablanca. Three of them were released on completion of their sentences. The other three were tied to their beds, each guarded by two policemen, and force-fed by naso-gastric tube for three years. By June 1989 they had gone into a coma again. This borders on the limits of the absurd. How can one still talk of 'life', what will be the permanent effects suffered by these young people after years of forced survival. If they don't die, can they ever rediscover a taste for life and eat normally? Doctors from AVRE[17] said in May 1989, 'These three young hunger strikers seem to us to represent a psychiatric emergency.'

These tragic events once again raise doubts about too narrow a view of medical intervention: if the doctor confines himself to a technical gesture, and reduces ethics to the protection of life at any price, he runs the risk of forgetting the essentially human character of his patient, and the latter's freedom of decision, even in detention. The idea of 'consent' to treatment, and of respect for the patient as a subject, takes on its full ethical meaning when a political will is at work. Maître Paley Vincent reminds us that 'if it is impossible to introduce the idea of permission to let a person die deliberately', it must be equally impossible to 'judge a man who, in full consciousness and not frivolously, idly or through miscalculation, has chosen to let himself die', or to maintain, as Dr Cohen Hadad does, that 'there is no such thing as a hunger strike'. As Dr Bernard Jomier says, who would have dreamed of force-feeding Mahatma Gandhi?

Pro-life mediator

The doctor should not, however, lose interest in the problem at the risk of becoming indifferent, which can sometimes cost the life of the hunger-striker (see box). In the conflict between the interests of authority, the duty to protect life, and the prisoner's dignity, it is important to 'establish a good doctor – patient relationship, which becomes fundamental in a hostile environment . . . With patience and persuasiveness, the doctor can play a useful part in the outcome, if he takes care that the authorities do not lose face and the prisoner does not lose his dignity' (Bernard Jomier). In Dr Pierre Espinoza's view:[18]

> in practice, the only way out when life is in danger is to work out a contract of care with an agreed time limit, under which the doctor, independently of the institutional power, proposes to act on a therapeutic level by starting a perfusion, while informing the highest administrative authorities of the seriousness of the patient's clinical condition and the uncertainties of the prognosis. This short-term contract allows a retreat from the danger zone, by giving those involved time to find a solution to the impasse.

If the doctor can maintain both his independence from the administration, and respect for confidentiality, and also refuse to act on a purely technical level by keeping a dialogue open,he can act as a genuine 'pro-life mediator' between the Devil and the deep blue sea.

Listening to a hunger striker

In 1988, COMEDE was responsible for taking care of Iranians on hunger strike in Paris. They were not deprived of their freedom, but we came up against a more general difficulty: after about thirty days, at the point where the physical condition becomes critical, it is hard to know whether they really want to continue, until death, or whether there comes a point when they want to stop. There is a sort of hunger striker's euphoria, even though he is aware that he is risking his life, which may give him a wish to die. The doctor must then be vigilant, and listen very closely, because there may be a moment when the hunger striker says he wants to stop. The doctor is in a very delicate position, poised between respect for the patient, and horror at watching someone die before his eyes. But there are moments when he can help the hunger striker, and he must do so.

Contribution by Dr Buisson-Touboul, President of COMEDE (Medical Committee for Aid to Exiles) (summary)

5 The death penalty and corporal punishment: an historical choice between abolition and medical involvement

'We live in a higher civilisation from this day,' Dr Southwick announced on 6 August 1890, after the execution of William Kemmler, the first man condemned to die by electrocution in New York.[1] Dr Southwick, a dentist and an opponent of execution by hanging, had developed the electrocution method, which was previously tested on animals. The Edison and Westinghouse companies, favouring the direct and the alternating current respectively, competed for the market in electric chairs. Associated Press quoted a doctor who witnessed the execution as saying that, as the first charge had been insufficient to kill the prisoner, a second had been administered. Edison, the electrician, then 'rebuked the doctors', according to Beichman,[2] and said it was 'a mistake to have let them handle the execution'.

The doctor and the electrician

Is an electrician whose technical skills facilitate an execution in any position to preach to a doctor whose technical skills are neither more nor less implicated in this killing? Emmanuel Maheu[3] says,

A doctor is basically a citizen, like anyone else, and I quite understand that his knowledge does not act as a vaccination against moral aberration, nor does it prevent him from following a primarily political ethic ... Yet even so, I am shocked that a doctor can torture anyone, because there is a humanist idea associated with medicine, which dates from long before the modern idea of human rights.

The difference between the electrician and the doctor is the difference between a profession with purely technical aims, and a group with its own system of ethics by which its members are entitled to lay hands on the human body in the interest of its welfare. When Dr Southwick proclaimed the 'higher degree of civilisation', he was not only hailing technical progress, but also the fact that the fundamental humanism of medicine was being applied to the death penalty. Just as the presence of a doctor beside the torturer almost instituted the practice of 'humane' torture in the UK, the implication of doctors in the death penalty has helped to justify its continued use.

In the beginning was torture. In the Middle Ages in Western Europe, the death penalty in its older versions was carried out in a particularly cruel and spectacular fashion: quartering, tying to the wheel and burning, were all preceded by diverse humiliations and mutilations. The style of execution was chosen to fit the crimes and personality of the convict. Modern States gradually certified the most cruel aspects of the death penalty illegal and instituted a version that was egalitarian, uniform, and quick. It was doctors who brought about this change, while Dr Guillotin himself was no more than an adviser. It was another doctor, a surgeon called Antoine Louis, who perfected the tool of the Terror. In Great Britain in 1885, doctors sat on a committee instructed to 'humanise' hanging. In the United States, after the electric chair, the gas chamber was introduced in Nevada in 1921, and lethal barbiturate injections have been given since 1977. Both these methods rely on medical knowledge. Thus, instead of insisting on the straightforward abolition of the right to put citizens to death, doctors have collaborated in bringing torment up to date. Yet the thousands of people who died during the Terror in France, the millions who died in the Nazi gas chambers, or the approximately 2,000 condemned people waiting on Death Row in American prisons on 1 May 1988, reveal the true character of this apparent progress.

At the height of the abolitionist tide in the USA, when executions had been suspended by the Supreme Court, the idea of lethal injections was put forward. There would be no screams and no smell, just people in white coats giving an injection, and someone drifting into unconsciousness and dying within minutes. This new 'clean' method of execution was also considered by British and French commissions, before capital punishment was finally abolished in Britain in 1969 and France in 1981. Today, with the United States Supreme Court authorising under-age and mentally-ill people to be condemned to death (see box), abolitionist movements are on the defensive. Doctors' involvement in execution has contributed to lifting the taboo.

---

14 July 1989

On 14 July 1989 Horace Dunkins, black, aged twenty-eight, was executed in Alabama by electrocution. He was convicted of the rape and murder in May 1980 of a white woman and sentenced to death in June 1981.

Owing to an error in the wiring of the electric chair, the first jolt of electricity failed to kill him. There was a delay of some nine minutes while the electric chair was reconnected and a second jolt of electricity was administered. Dunkins was pronounced dead nineteen minutes after the initial application of current. Two doctors are reported to have examined him after the first failed attempt and to have determined that he was unconscious but still had a strong heart beat.

Horace Dunkins was considered by the experts to be mentally retarded. He was the first person to be executed since June 1989 when the United States Supreme Court ruled in *Penry v. Lynaugh* that the execution of the mentally retarded was permissible under the US Constitution. In making this ruling, however, the Supreme Court said that mental retardation was a factor juries should consider when deciding whether to impose a death sentence. This did not happen in Horace Dunkins' case. According to an affidavit made by one of the jurors shortly before the execution, she would not have voted for a death sentence had she known of Horace Dunkins' retardation.

Since the US Supreme Court's ruling a month ago, a temporary stay of execution has been granted for a death row prisoner found to be mentally retarded in the state of Georgia.

Georgia enacted a law in 1988 to prohibit the execution of
the mentally retarded, and Maryland passed similar
legislation this year. The new laws do not apply retroactively
to prisoners already under sentence of death in the two states.
Some other states have recently considered similar legislation.

It has been estimated that 10% or more of the 2,200
prisoners under sentence of death in the USA may be
mentally retarded. In May 1989 the UN Economic and
Social Council adopted a resolution 'eliminating the death
penalty for persons suffering from mental retardation or
extremely limited mental competence, whether at the stage
of sentence or execution'.

Amnesty International, July 1989

Death on prescription, the final treatment

The doctor's responsibility is therefore involved and the
debate concerning medically controlled executions has at least
served to clarify the importance which the medical involvement plays in legitimising the death penalty. This phenomenon has acquired an unprecedented importance in the United
States where medical presence complements earlier religious
sources of legitimation. As we have already seen in some
States, psychiatrists would decide that some criminals were
'hopeless cases' without necessarily having met them, as in
the Barefoot case in July 1982. Nowadays, in some States
the psychiatric expert can be consulted three times over. The
first time, the individual has been convicted and the psychiatrist is asked to assess the responsibility of the accused. The
second time, before the punishment is passed, he has to judge
how 'dangerous' the criminal might be in future. The third
consultation is to judge whether the condemned person is
in a 'fit state' to be executed. Prisoners judged medically unfit
could initially be treated in psychiatric hospitals, until they
are considered cured and fit to be executed. This type of
assessment obviously causes endless disagreements among
the experts, especially as the convicts' condition fluctuates
all the time. The prospect of execution and the physical con-

ditions on Death Row generally make their mental state even worse.

Alvin Ford was condemned to death in 1975 at the age of twenty-two. In 1983, after eight years on Death Row, some experts considered him paranoid, others merely 'psychopathic', and his death sentence was definitively ruled against by the Supreme Court in 1986. Arthur Goode was not so 'lucky': he was executed in Florida on 5 April 1984, in spite of a psychiatric history that went back to the age of three. Morris Mason, executed in Virginia on 26 June 1985, was also an habitué of mental hospitals, where he had been judged schizophrenic and mentally retarded (according to his doctors, he had an IQ of 66 and a mental age of eight). Gary Alvord was condemned in 1973, spent ten years on Death Row, and was judged unfit three days before the date set for his execution. In the end several of the hospital staff refused, on ethical grounds, to care for him if it was only for the purpose of making him 'fit' to be put to death.

Here we have a psychiatrical ethic which considers that a patient cannot be made less dangerous but can be cured sufficiently to make him fit for execution. It is only one step from this to a situation where the death penalty becomes the final solution for hopeless psychiatric cases, i.e. a form of 'euthanasia'. The US Supreme Court seems to have taken that step in June 1989 in legalising the execution of mentally-ill people. While there is a theory that the death penalty often functions as a way out for a society whose socio-economic and education policies are unable to prevent violence, it would seem in this case to be a symptom of a psychiatric profession that has given up the attempts to provide options for its patients other than violence and death. Psychiatric legitimation of the death penalty seems to add a final justifying touch to a process of social exclusion: in the USA, as also in South Africa and Jamaica, the majority of the people condemned to death are black, poor, and illiterate. For a society powerless to cope with violence, or for a government incapable of negotiating with its opponents, the death penalty offers a solution. But the solution is both illusory, since it has no power as a unique deterrent, and immoral, since it is irreversible.[4]

The priest, the doctor, and 'Raison d'Etat'

The Inquisition made death the only possible outcome for some sinners; today it is the psychiatrist who is asked to take these decisions. Medical diagnosis has replaced religious disgrace. Indeed the one does not exclude the other, as the Buffet and Bontemp case showed in France.[5] The examining psychiatrists resorted to refined intellectual contortions to infer how dangerous the accused might be in future, though using the argument of his mental condition without shielding him from being sentenced: 'There are few forms of behaviour left to him today that match up to his self-image ... He killed in order to be true to himself.' His character was judged to be 'paranoid', but not at a 'pathological level' that would absolve him from criminal responsibility. Similarly, the Reverend Bruckberger, a Dominican priest close to President Pompidou, published an article in *France-Soir* a few days before the execution, at a point when a presidential pardon was still anticipated: 'If a criminal who has been condemned to death is deprived of the opportunity to go through with his punishment, this very often means he is deprived of the *only*[6] remaining means of being rehabilitated, even and especially in his own eyes.'

In other parts of the world, a certain number of Muslim countries have introduced so-called 'Islamic' punishments in the past few years: flogging, amputation of a hand or foot, and even 'crossed' amputation of one foot and one hand. In the Sudan, the military regime of President Numeiry introduced a scale of corporal punishments: for simple theft, amputation of the right hand; for armed or repeated robbery, amputation of the right hand and left foot; for adultery by an unmarried person, a hundred lashes; for adultery by a married person, death; for imbibing, manufacturing or possessing alcohol, a flogging of up to eighty lashes; and for taking part in an illegal gathering, fifteen to twenty-five lashes. Numerous floggings, and less frequent amputations, were carried out with the help of doctors or paramedical staff. Professor Ahmed, a Muslim mathematician and republican who was imprisoned for his opinions during that period, says that

Sudanese army doctors proved unwilling to co-operate, so prison warders were sent to Saudi Arabia to be trained in surgery and anaesthesia. On returning home, the Sudanese delegation allegedly announced that 'a special technique is required to amputate the hand at the wrist without causing excessive haemorrhaging and without damaging the bones'.[7]

In Mauritania, when doctors refused to co-operate, the authorities called in paramedical staff. In Pakistan, punishments of this kind were formerly used by the British colonial authorities, and were put back on the agenda in 1979. The law states that:

> The convict shall be medically examined by the authorised medical officer, so as to ensure that the execution of punishment will not cause the death of the convict. If the convict is ill, the execution of the punishment will be postponed ... The punishment shall be executed in the presence of a doctor ... If, after the punishment has begun, the authorised medical officer is of the opinion that there is a danger of death, the punishment shall be postponed.

Approval for corporal punishment is primarily religious, but a doctor's co-operation is also required. Iran is another country which requires this medical complicity. In November 1984 a police spokesman announced that, in collaboration with forensic experts, an amputation machine had been developed because amputation can pose medical problems and endanger the life of the convict. Paradoxically, the legal system here asks a doctor to guarantee death without 'torment', whereas elsewhere, the doctor is expected to maintain the torment, without death.[8] The paradox is a false paradox for in both cases, the doctor is needed to ensure that the procedure is carried out scientifically, and his approval seems indispensable to replace or reinforce the religious justification. Dr Alhoussayn Dia[9] says that when Mauritanian doctors went to see the President and argued that amputation is the job of the hangman, not the doctor, they were told that 'cutting off a hand is a way of treating the sickness of the soul, curing the person of his sins and curing society of a blemish'. In both cases the doctor is responsible to history. Abolition or medical involvement: that is the question.

In the opinion of Dr Mahboob Mehdi:[10]

> All those so-called 'Islamic' punishments are in fact pre-Islamic. The aim of those barbaric treatments is to terrorise the population and break its resistance. Whatever the technology (stoning, hanging, electrocution or injection) the aim is always to destroy life. There's nothing Islamic or un-Islamic in it. The problem is that most Islamic countries are either kingdoms or dictatorships or exploitative classes, which find it difficult to control the masses and are using the name of religion to break their resistance.

Dr Dia confirms this view:

> Islam arrived in societies where flogging, amputation, execution and inequality of the sexes were normal practice. Islam modified social custom and curbed the excesses. It is now up to us to ensure that any excesses that still persist in Islam should not be regarded as fundamental, on the same level as the Five Pillars of Islam. It's up to us, and here I'm speaking to my Muslim colleagues, to try and find the means within our law of toning down still further the practices that Islam began to modify centuries ago, bearing in mind the current universal awareness of human rights.

If unlawful: 'torture'. If lawful: 'legitimate punishment'

The World Medical Association resolved in 1981, 'that it is unethical for physicians to participate in capital punishment.' This declaration is very much in the spirit of traditional medical ethics, which are based on the protection of life and the integrity of the body. This interpretation is not universally accepted, however, and it actually shows a clear advance over international law, although the Universal Declaration of Human Rights proclaims the 'right to life'.

International humanitarian law (the Geneva Convention) protects prisoners against legal corporal punishments, including the death penalty, but it only covers situations of war and civil war. The United Nations Principles of Medical Ethics refer to the international law on the protection of human rights, which, in the 1975 Declaration against Torture, refuses to condemn 'pain or suffering arising only from, inherent in or incidental to, lawful sanctions'.

If unlawful: 'torture', if lawful: 'legitimate punishment'. The inclusion of this restrictive clause indicates in fact that corporal punishment and the death penalty are indeed 'cruel, inhuman and degrading'. Otherwise they would naturally have been included in the United Nations definition of torture, which is:

> any act by which severe pain or suffering, whether physical or mental, is intentionally inflicted by or at the instigation of a public official on a person for such purposes as obtaining from him or a third person information or confession, punishing him for an act he has committed or is suspected of having committed, or intimidating him or other persons.

When the writer, i.e. the member nations of the United Nations, adds that this 'does not include pain or suffering arising from ... lawful sanctions', the inadmissible is being admitted: thus, the United Nations consider that a court decision can make torture acceptable.

If hanging a person by the arms until he feels excruciating pain is rightly condemned as a act of torture, how should we view hanging him by the neck until he is dead? Putting 100-volt electric charges through a human body arouses indignation, yet 2,000 volts can legally be administered to a human being to kill him. An injection of a chemical substance that causes pain is an instrument of torture, but that is not the name for it when the dose is fatal. Physical and psychological marks on a victim are denounced as torture, but what about serious mutilation which inevitably causes humiliation and handicap? What about those people who are condemned to death and who live for years or even decades with the sentence hanging over them? Can it really be true that cruel methods used within a framework of legal procedure become 'humane' and 'legitimate'?

The physical and mental suffering entailed in execution cannot be measured. The press and non-governmental organisations regularly describe atrocious and prolonged executions. In Alabama in 1983, John Louis Evans had to be given three charges of 1,900 volts for fourteen minutes.

On 16 October 1985 in Indiana, Williem Vandiver's execution lasted seventeen minutes and took five electric charges. James Autry, executed on 14 March 1984, 'took at least ten minutes to die; for most of that time he was conscious, moving, and complaining that it hurt'. On 13 December 1988, Landry's execution lasted forty long minutes.

The threat of execution is one of the classic methods of torture. Condemnation to death is pronounced by a State, in the name of its people. If the condemned person benefits from judicial guarantees, he will have his torture prolonged, and be left suspended between the desire to live in hope and the necessity of preparing for what may be imminent death. Living in a state of total degradation, these prisoners oscillate between depression and elation, in conditions of detention that are almost always very harsh. All the studies carried out on these convicts[11] have shown that the prospect of death is painful and obsessive, and that there is a process of 'death of the personality' long before physical death. This includes physical and mental deterioration, loss of contact with the outside, and loss of a sense of reality – these symptoms are also typical of what happens to torture victims. In this context, the 'choice' given in some American states between different 'methods' of execution looks a macabre joke in itself fairly close to psychological torture methods. Doctors' involvement in the system can intensify this loss of a sense of reality. Some convicts find it more dignified to stand and face a firing squad than to set off as though for an operation, knowing they will never wake up.

There is a lack of data on the suffering associated with mutilations and other forms of corporal punishment. But everyone can imagine the humiliation associated with mutilation, a humiliation which sometimes seems to take the form of self-humiliation in a religious sense. Doctors are fully aware of the suffering and handicap that result from the mutilation of a hand or foot, even in other contexts. Loss of a limb or even a non-visible organ for medical reasons can be hard to cope with psychologically, and careful preparation and precautions are necessary before this type of operation. How can we imagine what it is like to be condemned by the State to have a healthy limb amputated which makes loss of control over one's body complete?

An absurdity

This absolute control over the body and the life of an individual is clearly a sign of insanity of that 'breakdown of any sense' which torture represents. It marks the point at which a State loses its reason and becomes totalitarian going against the most basic foundation of civilisation; the 'rights to life' plus the prohibition of torture are indeed of such importance that they appear right at the beginning of the universal Federation of Human Rights. Just as clinical opinion cannot ignore the cruelty of these acts, even when performed under anaesthetic, so medical ethics cannot, without becoming devoid of all sense, accept such a transgression. Death on prescription is meaningless, as a growing number of associations of health professionals have recognised; a conclusion which the international seminar 'Medicine at Risk' endorsed by consensus.

6 Punitive psychiatry and 'clean' torture

How can one define torture? In the opinion of all those who have experienced it, torture cannot be defined in thought or in words and represents inconceivable horror and madness. Long before the publication of the Compton Report or the beginning of experiments on sensory deprivation, human rights supporters had learnt to be wary of strictly physical definitions of torture. Even in cases of the most shocking brutality, the psychological aspects are always present and have been closely studied for many years. We have already seen how a psychiatric report can present political opponents or criminals as 'insane'. But far from simply condoning torture, psychiatrists and psychologists are now much more deeply involved. They have contributed to the insanity that characterises all torture — in the Soviet Union, Uruguay, Northern Ireland and Brazil in the past, and now in Pakistan and Chile. The development of methods of torture which are used to mask the facts and sidestep the taboo that surrounds torture have made a new global approach to the phenomenon a particularly urgent matter, without however having led to a satisfactory 'definition' of torture.

Anti-therapy 'methods'

There was an everyday kind of torture which consisted of a thought, a constant image that arose from what I saw around me in the psychiatric hospital: people out of touch with their surroundings. You say to yourself: that's what I may be like tomorrow. You begin to check up on yourself every morning, looking for the first signs of madness . . .

says Natalia Gorbanevskaya, a dissident who spent a year in a Soviet psychiatric hospital.[1] The vast, prolonged experiment in punitive psychiatry, spread over several decades in the Soviet Union and other Eastern Bloc countries, has done more than anything else to raise doubts about purely 'physical' definitions of torture. The testimonies of Dr Anatoly Koryagin and Nurse Alexander Podrabinek have described the way psychotropic drugs are used, often in cocktails: chlorpromazine (also known by its trade name, Largactil), haloperidol, and promazine. Large doses cause a string of unpleasant side-effects. Dr Drucker explains:[2]

> The greatest intensity of inhibitory effects is regarded as the appropriate result. The sedative effect is pursued to the point of stupor. This results in more or less massive disturbances in the train of thought, a positive destructuring of the mind ... On top of these direct effects there are also distressing sensations, which can be extremely painful.

Insulin therapy and very painful injections of sulfazine (elemental sulphur in oil), and more rarely electric shocks, are used as punishments. Apathy, headaches, psychomotor disorders, circulatory and hepatic disturbances, Parkinson's disease-like symptoms and acute depressive states, are some of the consequences of these forms of treatment.

The hospital system contributes to the destructuring of the individual through conditions of promiscuity with mental patients, blackmail and insults in the guise of psychotherapy, a ban on reading, writing and drawing, the lack of letters or visits, and uncertainty as to the date of release. The so-called 'special' Soviet psychiatric hospitals, which were veritable high-security prisons with military officers, used to represent[3] a concentration of all these methods. From experience, many victims have declared this regime to be worse than that of strict prison camps, which also use medical punishments, though to a lesser degree. In all cases, the accounts irresistibly evoke the concentration camps, except that instead of scientifically-organised massacre, the aim is to cause madness.

'We didn't liquidate them when we had the chance. Now we must make the most of the time we have left to drive them mad,' announced the former director of Uruguay's Libertad prison, Major Maciel. During the nine years of the military dictatorship, he was directly assisted by a psychologist, Dr Britos, who appeared to the prisoners to be the real boss. According to former prisoners, inmates were taken repeatedly to his fifth-floor office, an oasis of luxury in the bleak prison environment, where they underwent various psychological tests to assess their aggressive tendencies, sexuality, sources of anxiety and defence mechanisms. Throughout their years in confinement, the prisoners were taken to his office for any act that was considered violent, in addition to the immediate penalty (change of floor, solitary confinement, withdrawal of visiting rights). Through this subtle blend of psychiatric attention and violence, they were 'amicably' encouraged to let drop a few confidences about themselves or their fellow-inmates. The information obtained from these interviews, along with tape recordings of family visits and the 'files' passed on by the prisoners' former torturers, allowed Dr Britos and his team to develop 'personalised' forms of treatment. In the women's prison, Punta de Rieles, other doctors operated in the same way.[4]

'If a prisoner had a family visit and showed the slightest sign of anxiety or annoyance about his children, he would be summoned in the next few days. Britos would come over as kind and condescending. Very often, after that interview, the prisoner would be moved to a different cell, and put in with someone who had psychiatric problems,' David Campora remembers. 'Our friends Danilo Sequeira and Tito Gonzalez were taken to the *Isla* [disciplinary quarters] for three months' isolation, accused of homosexuality. Tito was given Calmancial. Britos went there to persuade them personally to sign a document admitting their "offence",' says Charles Serralta. And Miguel Angel Estrella says, 'It was obvious to us that Britos had a hand in the selective organisation of the cells, whenever we felt there was a determination to destroy a particular inmate. In that case, they would put people together who were very different, politically and as individuals.'

Any suicide attempt was used to gain the prisoner's collaboration, with the help of strong doses of neuroleptics. Cia Del Campo, an acute psychotic according to his fellow-prisoners, was tortured several times, and regularly summoned for nocturnal interrogation sessions. Antonio Mas Mas was exposed for years to an arbitrary alternation of punishments, violent 'medical treatment' (electric shocks, strong doses of neuroleptics), and total neglect accompanied by sudden withdrawal of psychotropic drugs. His experiences are fairly representative of psychological and psychiatric torture spread over a period of years.

While chlorpromazine and sulfazine symbolised Soviet punitive psychiatry, the drug that spread fear throughout Libertad was Calmancial (fluphenazine 300 mg, with delayed effect). In high doses, its effect is to produce 'extra-pyramidal symptoms',[5] vegetative and eyesight disorders, and in some cases, coma. 'It must have been thirty minutes before I began to feel itchy all over and a lump in my throat. I had violent palpitations, my lower jaw went stiff. I sat down on the floor, I couldn't think about anything ... I began to have awful pain in the joints ...', says one prisoner. 'He couldn't talk or co-ordinate his movements. His face didn't look human. After a few weeks, as the effects of the drug wore off, he turned out to be very intelligent and really good company. You could talk to him quite easily about anything,' says another.

Pharmaceutical products, and precise manipulation of the affective and sensory environment, have become methods of torture. This may be happening in a concerted way:[6] apart from local particularities, the same methods of torture have been revealed in six Latin American countries. They comprise pharmacological manipulation – psychotropic drugs, LSD and other hallucinogens, and muscle-paralysing drugs such as curare; the classic physical methods of electric shock, deprivation or forced ingestion, fixed positions, mutilations; and also sensory manipulation – deprivation of sleep, sensory isolation, enforced stimuli (lights or noises); manipulation of relationships through isolation or overcrowding, prohibited or perverted contacts with others, being forbidden to speak, or having communication forced on one, or limited. There are also the psychological methods: uncertainty about one's fate, fake releases and simulated executions, threatened or actual violence against relatives, and various types of humiliation.[7]

A good many of these methods are universal and ancient, but medical techniques have meant they can be systematised. Enforced holding of a fixed position, for example, has been in practice for a very long time and is not the direct result of new developments in the understanding of physiology, although these do allow a better mastery of it. Manipulation of the mind is at the very basis of the torture mechanism, but it has been refined by a more precise knowledge of psychology. Finally, isolation, the universal sign of torture, has developed as an antitherapy by moving into the sensory field. Its use is encouraged by the concern to leave no marks.

Isolation and its after-effects

An Iranian political prisoner who was released in 1982 says:[8]

> The worst thing in Evin is being held blindfold for days on end, waiting for someone to tell you why you are there. Some people are left blindfold for days, weeks or months. One man spent 27 months like this. None of the prisoners appears to know what he is being held for. After 27 months, he sits, largely in total silence, nodding his head from one side to the other. Sometimes he just sits knocking his head on the wall.

So many accounts by people who have been tortured begin with the words 'I was kept blindfolded'. Torture always means being held in secret, cut off from the outside world. As the hood and the blindfold show, it also means more or less elaborate and rigorous sensory isolation. Advances in bio-medical knowledge and experiments in psycho-physiology have cast light on the vulnerability of the human organism and thought process to this type of treatment. Dr Timothy Shallice[9] stresses the similarities between the methods used in 1971 by the British Army in Northern Ireland and the much slower ones used by the KGB in the 1930s. 'This development [in methods of interrogation] was completed by applying the results of scientific research into sensory deprivation carried out in the 1950s. Something that used to take six weeks now only takes six days.' He considers that the KGB methods 'were the optimum development of skilled methods without direct physical violence before the introduction of ideas acquired through scientific research ... The points the two techniques have in common are isolation, deprivation of sleep, vague threats, depersonalisation, bad diet and alterations in temperature.'

'The prosecutor acknowledged that the cells were uniformly painted gleaming white and that, on the orders of the examining magistrate, the light was left on twenty-four hours out of twenty-four.'[10] In the Federal Republic of Germany, as in Northern Ireland and Spain, techniques of isolation have become more sophisticated. Contemporary prison architecture has reached heights of visual, acoustic and tactile monotony, particularly sought after in the isolation quarters. Police methods exploit research into sleep rhythms. In the early 1970s in Brazil, Dr Amilcar Lobo learnt that new methods of torture were being tried out in the barracks:

> They told me it was a British formula, copied from Scotland Yard. There was one completely dark cell, and one painted white. Neither of them had windows. The prisoner would be given lunch and then locked up in the dark cell and given something to put him to sleep, probably a barbiturate. After a few hours he would be woken up and given lunch again to make him think a whole day had gone by. If he didn't talk, he would be put back in the dark cell with a loud noise for several hours, and then interrogated again. If he still wouldn't talk, he would be put in the white-painted cell with a blinding light.

Constant or manipulated light causes loss of temporal references, and the biological clock is de-regulated by changing sleep patterns and mealtimes. Spatial references are lost through uniformity of the environment, or hooding. Then there can be sensory loss and loss of any sense of relationship with the outside world and with others (see box on p. 67). Whatever their theoretical approaches, the different experiments on sensory isolation carried out in laboratory conditions have shownthat serious disturbances can occur within

Between four walls

Alongside hard, brutal torture, there are other forms of constraint that are more insidious and more hypocritical but no less capable of breaking down an opponent and annihilating his will. This is true, for example, of isolation. It is increasingly being used by regimes that govern through terror because it allows them to destroy a personality rapidly without leaving too many traces. Biologists now know that living systems have to be used in order to keep going. Otherwise they deteriorate, wither away and decay. Within a few weeks, a man in complete isolation who is tied up and blindfolded with his ears blocked, loses control of his own body. He no longer has words, ideas or concepts. He no longer has points of reference to balance his gestures and his thoughts. He falls prey to hallucinations. He feels guilty. He becomes totally vulnerable, with no link to his family, cut off from his friends and his past. Exhausted and anguished, he is at the mercy of his jailers.

Life like this between four walls, in darkness, in silence, and in total ignorance, is worse than the life of a dog chained to his kennel. There are men who treat other men worse than you would treat a dog. They do this to frighten them – to annihilate, discredit, cancel out and crush them, to dehumanise the human qualities in their opponents. We must fight against this form of violence that degrades human beings, both those who suffer it and those who put it into practice. We must denounce torture that deals no blows or bruises but destroys people just as effectively as the other kind.

Professor François Jacob, *Cahiers de la commission médicale*, no. 4, Amnesty International, French Section, July 1985

hours[11] in, for example, intellectual performance (difficulties in concentration, co-ordination, interpretation and remembering), perception (to the point of multiple hallucinations), self-perception (sense of unreality or floating), and mood (aggression, anxiety, euphoria, depression). These experiments corroborate the testimonies of ex-prisoners: 'You see

yourself changing . . . becoming paranoid, staring at the walls
. . . talking to the ants, hallucinating, and never being able
to measure the extent of these deviations and the damage
they were causing because you have nothing to compare yourself with . . . Isolation made me sick of myself and other
people,' says Breten Breytenbach.[12] 'You go from despair to
exhaustion, from exhaustion to a sort of emptiness, a deep,
gnawing emptiness which atrophies you. At this stage, anything that can happen to a human being is unforeseeable,' Eva
Forest writes.[13] In Franco's Spain she experienced the kind
of torture 'that mutilates a person without touching the body,
and enables the person who perpetrates it to feign surprise
when he's criticised, and say cynically: "I don't understand
what you're talking about. We don't ill-treat anyone here."'

Yet isolation does leave traces. 'International studies in cri-
minology and psychology indicate that isolation can in itself
have serious effects on the physical and psychological constitution: chronic apathy, debility, emotional fragility, difficulty
in concentration, disturbances to the neuro-vegetative system,' the European Commission on Human Rights reported
in 1976, referring to the conditions of detention of political
prisoners in West Germany.[14] A medical examination showed
that one of the German women prisoners had 'a general lowering of arterial pressure, accompanied by very clear disturbances to the peripheral circulation, with impairment of the
immune system and a state of marked exhaustion of the neuro-
vegetative system'. The tribunal then accepted that 'according
to the medical report, the accused woman's cardio-vascular
system cannot be put in order, even if the place and conditions
of detention are changed'. Amnesty International received
a statement from Professor Rash, saying that one of the Red
Army Faction prisoners, Werner Hoppe, was vomiting everything he ate and drank, and suffering from internal haemorrhaging and sharp pains in the shoulder. The doctor considered
recovery 'unlikely even after his release'.

In the early 1970s, Professor Robert Daly[15] examined former Irish prisoners who had undergone the methods of 'strict
discipline and isolation'. He considered that 'almost all of
them' showed signs of obvious psychic weakness. The com-

monest symptoms were anxiety or terror, as in nightmares or startle reactions. Almost all of them had suffered from depression.

'Demolition' or the impossible knowledge

We touch here on the absurdity of the distinction between torture and strict isolation, or psychological and physical torture. 'Sensory' torture causes deterioration in the psyche, and 'psychological' torture causes lasting somatic disorders. In fact, it is always the whole person who is affected. 'You can't say psychic assault is more or less serious; torture is a single entity,' Dr Nicole Léry explains.[16] 'What you can say is that you meet victims long afterwards who have been drained of their selves, who are alone and who can no longer bear the caresses of their partner or the shouts of their children. They break into a sweat if they hear an object falling, and are incontinent at the slightest emotion. Even if they've recovered from their cigarette burns and their broken bones.'

'Psychiatric repression,' Dr Ian Vianu[17] echoes, 'is neither more nor less vile than any other kind. It's a way of imposing silence.' In both cases, the other person's mind becomes the absolute enemy, reduced to a label of 'schizo-divergent' or 'subversive enemy of the fatherland'. In both cases, as psychoanalyst Marcello Vignar explains,[18] 'totalitarian barbarity uses highly-developed methods based on one fundamental truth: the primacy of a man's relationship with his own body'. 'It isn't the repertoire of different forms of violence that's important. The essential organising elements are infinite time, unlimited horror, isolation, strangeness, loneliness, and a succession of fragmented contradictory messages which lead to madness in the sensory deprivation syndrome ...' To Dr Miguel Benasayag, 'Torture only works because there is isolation, which implies the absolute shattering of the prisoner's self.'[19]

Whatever methods are used, the torturer's aim is always the same – to bring the prisoner to the point where the personality shatters, the 'experimental psychosis, in which there is no other person, only a sort of fusion, when the victim is glued to the torturer', Dr Benasayag says. Marcello Vignar, adopting the expression of a patient who was a torture victim, calls it 'the point of demolition'. Separated from all his reference points and his previous identity, when his broken body is at the torturer's mercy, and as in a nightmare, the victim may see no outcome other than submitting to the only other person available, the torturer. Pain and sensory deprivation entail the same dependence. In any case, Dr Benasayag explains, the subject is 'no longer there'. He is caught in 'a huge transference towards the torturer ... The torturer is all-powerful and omniscient, and you are nothing but an insignificant or partial object'.[20] In this chaos, anything can happen: the victim 'talks' more or less, or gives answers which miss the point. Pepe, one of Dr Vignar's patients, clung to a heroic hallucination to keep himself from talking.

In every case, the event leaves marks, which may or may not be overcome. The Austrian philosopher Jean Amery, who was tortured by the Gestapo, wrote:[21]

> Once tortured, always tortured ... A person who has been through torment will never be able to live again in the world as his natural habitat. The abomination of annihilation can never be extinguished. One's faith in humanity, which was bruised as soon as the first blow was struck, and then demolished by torture, can never be regained.

Without necessarily sharing his pessimism, many witnesses have spoken of the suffering but also the shame that mark the survivors of torture or the concentration camps. The irrational shame of 'being alive in someone else's place', of having had to adhere, however briefly, to the system or to the torturer in order to survive, pursues the victims for a long time, even those who managed not to talk.[22] Tito de Alençear, a young Dominican friar who was tortured in 1969, killed himself in 1974. His doctor, Jean Claude Rolland,[23] said he was unable to bear the loss of self-respect, a feeling 'which is "impervious" to any reasonable argument, and results from the compromise the victim has to make when he is forced into an attachment to his torturer'.

Torture is chaos, madness, psychosis and regression: it is in any event that which 'one cannot know'. This is the impression we get from those who have lived through it but cannot talk about it. With how many blows, how many hours spent alone or standing up, or without sleep, does torture begin? This is unforseeable, as are also its long term effects. Nor is it more possible to draw a 'nosography' of different types of torture. However, such an ascendancy over the individual, such a systematic destruction of a person's beliefs, identity and humanity, and the resulting terror spread throughout a whole society, are the apanage of a totalitarian system, whatever tools it may employ. To allow it to be thought that such a result could be obtained by painless, because medicalised, methods would be tantamount to reducing torture to the level of a banality by giving it an aura of respectability. Doctors will be held back from the impossible attempt to 'humanise' torture, less by a clinical approach to the subject than by this, namely that the horror of torture can never be known.

7 Medical ethics and resistance to torture

The Vicaría de la Solidaridad is a Catholic human rights organisation which runs a clinic in Santiago, Chile. On 15 February 1989, Mr Torres, the military prosecutor, went to the clinic to seize the medical records of 5,000 people. But the files had disappeared, and Bishop Sergio Valech refused to say where they were. This was one more episode in a long-running conflict between the Vicaría and the Chilean authorities which began after an assault on a bakery in 1986. One of the participants was injured and was taken to the clinic for treatment. Both Dr Ramiro Olivares, the Vicaría's senior doctor, and a Vicaría lawyer were charged with 'covering up a terrorist offence'. The tribunal demanded information from the Vicaría on its organisation and staff, and also on the identity of people treated at the clinic, especially those with bullet wounds. The Vicaría handed over information that did not affect medical confidentiality, but lodged a complaint against the prosecutor, as he was asking for information that had no bearing on the original offence. The court found in the Vicaría's favour, but was overruled on 28 December 1988 by the Supreme Court.

This case is not unique. On 9 and 10 May 1989, the South African security police raided the Durban headquarters of the anti-apartheid medical and dental association NAMDA, two days before its annual congress was due to begin. They seized case records and computer files. The Durban office co-ordinates NAMDA's work on behalf of former detainees from all over South Africa. This violation of medical confidentiality risked making released detainees too frightened to use NAMDA's community treatment centres in future.

The 1970s marked the beginning of a significant new awareness of human rights among health professionals, which has continued over the years. There was a memorable event in 1975, when the Tokyo Declaration by the World Medical Association supported British doctors in their refusal to condone torture in Northern Ireland. That same year, the United Nations adopted a Declaration on the Protection of All Persons from being Subjected to Torture, and the International Council of Nurses produced a very firm and precise declaration on 'The role of the nurse in the care of detainees and prisoners'. This objects to any participation in cruel treatment or even in the maintenance of order in a prison, and stated, 'the nurse's first responsibility is towards her patients, notwithstanding considerations of national security and interest'. In Hawaii in 1977, the World Psychiatric Organisation adopted a code of ethics 'to prevent misuse of psychiatric ideas, skills and technology'. In 1977 it also denounced the abuse of psychiatry in the Soviet Union and set up a committee to examine complaints. In February 1983, after several years of effort on the part of European psychiatric associations to send a mission to the USSR, the Soviet Association of Neurologists and Psychiatrists withdrew from the World Psychiatric Association, three months before the Vienna congress.

Alongside these international achievements, the ethical movement has brought together a strong minority of doctors within many separate countries. They treat the victims of civil war and repression, mount individual or joint protests against violations of medical ethics, and support doctors and nurses who have been repressed for taking a stand. As these movements have become more structured, they have drafted codes of conduct, set up committees to collect evidence and instigate sanctions against doctors who breach such codes, and organised treatment centres. They take risks, and have scored some successes.

Dissident prison doctors

'When I went to work at San Quentin prison, which houses the Death Row and the gas chamber in California, I made it clear to the physician chief hiring me that I was against the death penalty and would not be willing to participate in executions,' says Dr Kim Marie Thorburn, a doctor in the American prison service. 'He said, fine, but it turned out he probably didn't have the say in the matter. That it was going to be the prison administration that would make that determination. It is the prison administration's opinion in the State of California that this is a function of prison physicians since it's a regulation in California that two doctors are to be present and that they'll call on the prison doctors in turn to participate ... We didn't have an execution, but I was threatened with sanctions because of my outspoken position against the death penalty.'

Resistance often begins at an individual level, when a doctor or nurse 'caught in the storm' takes the solitary decision to say no. A young Danish volunteer was sent to an African country by a non-governmental aid organisation and suddenly found himself called on to declare a prisoner 'fit' to be flogged. He refused, quoting the Tokyo Declaration. There was no major risk to him personally, as he was protected by his status as a foreigner, but the situation proved impossible to resolve. The prisoner could not be freed until he had actually been punished, and he himself asked the doctor to authorise his punishment. The volunteer could find no other solution than to leave the country.

That solution would be impossible in most cases. Dr Juan Villegas, head of the serious burns unit in a hospital in Santiago, Chile, was held responsible for the publication of a press report on the sufferings of one of his female patients, Carmen Quintana, and was dismissed in July 1988. A Romanian prison doctor, Attila Kun, refused to 'cover up' incidents of torture, and was sent to prison for three years.

In Leningrad, psychiatrist Marina Voykhanskaya became progressively aware of abuses of psychiatry, and increasingly exposed herself to repression. In April 1974 she received a patient who was labelled 'schizophrenic' despite an unusually inconclusive case record. He had already spent a year in a mental institution and been treated with massive doses of haloperidol. She found out later that Anatol Dimitrievitch Ponomarov had come to the notice of the authorities in 1968 for making critical comments about the invasion of Czechoslovakia at a local Party meeting, and then in 1970 because he was reading foreign literary magazines.

Smelling a rat, I decided to take a risk. 'Anatol Dimitrievitch,' I said, feeling like a heroine or some great moral character, 'it's hard for me to tell whether you're sick or not. Let's make a deal. I'm going to stop the treatment. If you aren't ill, you will behave calmly. If I hear any complaints from the nurses, that will mean you *are* ill, and whether you like it or not we will have to carry on with the treatment.' I then saw a flicker of warmth in his eyes, and he agreed silently. Of course, there were no incidents.[2]

Marina Voykhanskaya was put under KGB surveillance, and demoted. In 1975 she managed to leave the country. Irina Koroleva and Vladimir Moskalkov, who were doctors at the Sytchiovska psychiatric prison, were dismissed in 1975. Olga Makarova, Anatoly Barabanov, and many others, were themselves sent to mental hospitals. Dr Semyon Gluzman, who had refused to certify General Grigorenko as schizophrenic in 1972, was sent to the Perm camp, where with mathematician Bukovsky he co-authored a 'Manual of psychiatry for political dissidents'. The last thing to do, they advised their readers, 'is to stress one's moral worth' during a psychiatric examination. Rather, one should do the opposite: 'Claim to have got involved without weighing up the consequences, and in the hope of glory.' If they were still sent to psychiatric hospital in spite of all their efforts, they should 'use all your guile to persuade the psychiatrist that your political opinions have evolved'.

In 1977, opposition to punitive psychiatry became more organised. In the aftermath of attempts to put the 1975 Helsinki Agreement into effect, a 'Working committee to investigate the use of psychiatry for political purposes' was set up, largely on the initiative of Nurse Alexander Podrabinek. As an ambulance driver in Moscow for several years, Podrabinek had transported a good many dissidents to psychiatric hospitals. From 1973 onwards he had been collecting material for his book *Punitive Medicine* which was published in 1977 as *samizdat*.[3] The committee gathered and circulated information, provided legal advice, and interceded in hospitals on behalf of dissidents. They began to apply pressure both inside and outside the country, most importantly by preparing a dossier for the Sixth World Congress of Psychiatrists in Honolulu, which was to condemn psychiatric abuses. Because of their activities there were more arrests, this time Dr Leonard Tanovsky and Dr Anatoly Koryagin. A few years later, in the current climate of *perestroika*, the committee along with Alexander Podrabinek and Dr Gluzman, as well as the International Association Against the Political Use of Psychiatry, are still keeping a close watch on Soviet psychiatry and encouraging change.[4]

'Voices against torture'

The torture debate flared up again in Britain in 1977. Doctors at Castlereagh Central Police Station and Gough Barracks, after numerous attempts at dialogue, informed the administration that they had observed evidence of ill-treatment and would resign unless something was done to put a stop to it. They quoted the European Commission on Human Rights.[5] During the same period, Amnesty International sent a research team to Northern Ireland. Although the situation improved considerably, signs of ill-treatment reappeared a few months later. Dr Elliott, senior doctor at Gough, and four of his colleagues, wrote to the police authorities, with the support of the Association of Forensic Medical Officers. On 21 April 1978, the police commissioner gave the order to instal spy-holes in the doors of the interrogation rooms at Gough to allow surveillance. In 1979 the report of an independent commission showed how effective measures of protection could be implemented.

In the early 1980s, health workers mobilised against torture in many Latin American countries, and in the Philippines, Mauritania, South Africa and Egypt. Their efforts are often linked to 'primary' or 'community' health care for poor sectors of the population. During civil war (as in Central America), or under highly repressive military dictatorships (Chile or Argentina), or under regimes that are both discriminatory and violent (like South Africa), the state of health care tends to be as neglected as the concern for human rights. Doctors become involved in the political, social or humanitarian field, as well as in their professional practice. This quite naturally leads them to treat the victims of repression, and so to suffer repression themselves in the process. In El Salvador, soldiers carried out raids on hospitals, abducting members of the medical staff and murdering them. Doctors who have died and 'disappeared' can be counted in double figures, both in El Salvador and in Guatemala. In India, doctors associated with the feminist and civil rights movements lose their jobs. In 1989, health workers in community groups in the Philippines were still being harassed by the military and by unofficial militia groups, who accused them of treating rebels. The Manila 'Medical Action Group' organised support for the health workers. In July 1988, the Philippine Nurses' Association proclaimed its support for those people who were exercising 'the right to treat any patient irrespective of his or her social status or political opinions'.

One by one, major professional associations have begun to take a stand against doctors' participation in torture, basing their arguments on the Tokyo Declaration. In Chile, the Colegio Médico (representing 98 per cent of the profession) has committed itself to this struggle and has paid heavily in terms of imprisonment and internal banishment. According to the Colegio, 284 doctors have been imprisoned or killed since 1973. The Turkish Medical Association has protested against torture and executions, and several of its members have been imprisoned. But professional representative bodies which may be linked to the political powers often remain passive, and so numerous spontaneous groups have been set up in response to an urgent need. In South Africa, the affair of Steve Biko's doctors was referred to the SAMDC (South African Medical and Dental Council, the disciplinary body of the profession) by the Council of Churches. The SAMDC buried the file, with the approval of MASA, which is officially an independent association but is very close to the government. In the end it was a Supreme Court decision that decreed the two doctors should stand trial. According to the report by the American Association for the Advancement of Science in 1987, 'The failure of the SAMDC and MASA to respond quickly and appropriately to the allegations against the Biko doctors had resulted in a bitter international controversy within the World Medical Association concerning MASA's membership.' In 1981, the British Medical Association resigned from the WMA. In South Africa, doctors opposed to apartheid formed NAMDA in 1982.

The Syrian Medical Association demanded in 1980 an end to the 'terror' and the abolition of emergency tribunals. The national medical association in Egypt has also protested against doctors' participation in torture and asked in vain for means of investigation. In Algeria, an anti-torture medical committee was set up in January 1989. In Pakistan, Dr Mahboob Mehdi and his colleagues have organised an inter-disciplinary forum, Voices Against Torture, which has called on the Pakistani Medical Council to readopt the terms of the Tokyo Declaration, and has protested about amputations and floggings (see box). Similarly, in Mauritania and the Sudan, doctors have refused to take part in amputations.

Pakistani voices

In Pakistan, doctors' participation in torture is considered one of their professional duties. It takes the following forms:

* Under the Execution of the Punishment of Whipping Ordinance of 1979:

> Before the execution of punishment commences, the convict shall be medically examined by the authorised medical officer, so as to ensure that the execution of punishment will not cause the death of the convict. If the convict is ill, the execution of the punishment shall be postponed until the convict is certified by the authorised medical officer to be physically fit to undergo the punishment. The punishment shall be executed in the presence of the authorised medical officer, at such public places as the Provincial Government may appoint for the purpose. If after the execution of the punishment has commenced the authorised medical officer is of the opinion that there is apprehension of the death of the convict, the execution of the punishment shall be postponed . . .

* In many interrogation centres, the person to be interrogated is examined by the doctor and declared fit for interrogation.
* The conduct of the prison medical officer in most of the cases is very unethical and falls very short of the United Nations declarations and code of ethics. Instead of providing standard and best available treatment to the prisoners, the prison medical officers usually behave as part of the prison administration and take part in torture.
* Cover-up activities by some doctors, such as providing false death certificates, or false clinical records of the victims torture is very common.
* If the court orders amputation of hand or foot as punishment to someone, then according to the law, it will be carried out only by an authorised medical officer personally.

I have interviewed men and women who were tortured in different torture chambers and prisons of Pakistan. These victims have given evidence about the participation of doctors in the process of torture. One of the victims interviewed himself was a doctor and he faced his own class-fellow doctor in the torture chamber. Usually these doctors: a) advise the torturers about the actual conditions of the victim's health; b) revive the victims sufficiently to undergo further torture. Torture was always endemic in Pakistan, but during the last decade it reached epidemic proportions. In Pakistan authorities often tried to legitimise many kinds of torture by taking the cover of religion. Due to this reason, we are using the Declaration of Tokyo along with the Declaration of Kuwait which says 'the medical profession shall not permit its technical, scientific or other resources to be utilised in any sort of harm or destruction or the infliction upon man of physical, psychological, moral or other damage, regardless of all political or military considerations.'

Dr Mahboob Mehdi, founder of Voices Against Torture,
at the "Medicine at Risk" conference (summary)

'Direct or indirect participation in an execution is a perversion of medical ethics,' says the American Psychiatric Association, which is campaigning against medical reports that predict 'dangerousness' in capital cases. The American Medical Association announced in 1980 that the doctor's only association with the death penalty should be to certify death. The American Nurses' Association ruled out all involvement in 1983. The WMA declaration on the death penalty in 1981 set off a flood of similar resolutions: from the Secretary-General of the Brazilian Medical Association, all the Scandinavian medical associations, and the Australian Medical Association.

Ethical tribunals

The doctors and nurses who belong to these associations often produce detailed papers and valuable medical ethics. Their definition of torture generally includes the death penalty and corporal punishment. Rules on the treatment of detainees are often dealt with in detail, as in the British and Pakistani documents. The associations try to influence official professional bodies in the hope of securing action against offenders and preventive regulation. The Turkish Medical Association mounted a campaign in 1989 to persuade the government to integrate its views into the official code. It decided on the expulsion of six torturing doctors, but this measure was later cancelled by the Turkish courts. In Chile, where the Colegio Médico is independent and comprises the majority of the profession, forty-two dossiers on doctors associated with torture were investigated, and eight doctors were expelled from the Colegio after a fair and proper 'hearing'. Of course, a decision of this kind carries no legal weight, but its political and moral weight is immense. 'Since we adopted this code and applied these sanctions,' says Dr Francisco Rivas,[6] 'a lot of doctors have left the army, or refused to do any more work for the security services. Most of the doctors we expelled, even if they were army doctors, have lost their jobs or become marginalised in the profession.'

In July 1984, the Uruguayan national medical convention provided an opportunity to denounce doctors who had taken part in torture under the military dictatorship, which ended peaceably in 1985. Investigations into human rights violations

which occurred during the twelve years of the Junta were hanging fire, the civilian powers had their hands tied, and the
exactions by the military were still going on. The medical
profession showed its determination to see the guilty brought
to account by setting up a National Commission of Medical
Ethics. On 27 October 1984, Dr Eduardo Saiz Pedrini was
expelled from the medical body by an extraordinary professional tribunal set up by the provincial Medical Federation.
He was found guilty of issuing a mendacious certificate to
cover up the death under torture of Dr Vladimir Roslik on
16 April of the same year.

On 4 March 1985 the Uruguayan National Commission
of Medical Ethics began to function. Prisoners were freed,
testimonies poured in, and the extent of the horror was unco-
vered, as also was the extent to which doctors were involved.
On the basis of international law and international rules of
ethics, the commission developed a procedure for evaluating
the charges. It examined about a hundred cases, a small
number of which resulted in expulsion from the professional
organisations.

'If we take into account the gravity of these lapses, we ought
not to be dealing simply with ethics but with criminal justice,'
said Dr Rodolfo Shurmann, a medico-legal expert and member of the National Commission of Medical Ethics. But the
matter could not be referred to the courts, as an amnesty
law was passed in December 1986. It guaranteed immunity
to members of the armed forces and police (including doctors)
who had been obeying orders or acting from political motives.
The only exception, which did not have any concrete results,
concerned people who were responsible for disappearances.
Several doctors were very active in 1989 in the referendum
campaign to repeal the amnesty law. The referendum failed
on 16 April 1989 (with 40 per cent of the votes against immunity) and one of the most committed doctors, Dr Gregorio
Martirena, had to cope with a libel action brought by Judge
Raggio in July 1989. Referring to the death of Dr Roslik,
the judge apparently tried to discourage Dr Martirena from
taking any legal action, asking him why he was going to so
much trouble over a dead man.

The issue hung fire in Argentina as well. In the scramble of the military government's departure, under pressure from many sources, Dr Jorge Bergès, the obstetrician and convicted torturer, was condemned to six years in prison on 2 December 1986. But in June 1987 Argentina passed its own 'law of forgetting', under which all the executive agents responsible for torture and thousands of 'disappearances' were exempt from standing trial on the grounds of their 'duty to obey'. Dr Bergès was released, along with 300 other condemned torturers. Medical groups and human rights associations then set up an 'ethical tribunal' in spite of threats and intimidation. The professional bodies, however, have not followed their lead.

Treatment centres

In certain countries, including those that take in refugees, treatment is being organised for the victims of repression. Torture, which produces intense and complex reactions, poses a wide range of problems for the doctor in terms of examination and reporting as well as therapy. It is hard to prove that a burn, or a head trauma, or a partial or total paralysis, were caused by ill-treatment. Many doctors suffer from 'professional myopia'[7] and show no interest in the causes of the traumas they observe. The after-effects of torture are not exclusively physical; they can also be psychosomatic or psychological. It is not only the direct victims who are affected, but also their children, relatives and friends. Society as a whole may need treatment for the fear and self-blame that result from torture.

In Argentina, even under the dictatorship, the Mothers of the Plaza de Mayo started a psychological counselling service for the families of the '*desaparecidos*' who were faced with unbearable suspended bereavement. After the return to civilian government, this project was developed further. Individual therapy and group work were established, often with professional help. In the Philippines, the Medical Action

Group has set up a service for torture victims and, more recently, a specialised centre for children.

The countries that take in refugees – Australia, Canada, the United States, France, Denmark, the Netherlands, Great Britain – have various structures for helping torture victims. In France, treatment is given in multi-purpose outpatients' clinics as well as by bodies specifically devoted to refugees: these are COMEDE (Comité medical pour les exilés) and AVRE (Association pour les Victimes de la Répression en Exil). AVRE has set up an independent care unit in the Saint-Simon hospital in Paris, where a multi-disciplinary team has cared for about 500 patients and their families. AVRE has also sent fact-finding missions abroad, the most recent of which was in 1989 on behalf of several Moroccan hunger strikers.

The International Centre for the Rehabilitation of Torture Victims was set up in Copenhagen in 1982. As well as its intense and varied therapeutic activity, it has taken part in numerous evaluative missions and is involved in doctors' training all over the world and in research into the physiological and psychological after-effects of torture. It now publishes an international quarterly newsletter.[8]

Help for the victims of repression is not a question of simple neutral skill any more than the involvement of doctors in torture is. As Dr Hélène Jaffé of AVRE says, 'Many doctors can recognise the traces of torture,' yet they say nothing. Both the evidence which doctors can give of the ill-treatment which patients have suffered and the care they provide are a statement to society and to international authorities. One step in the healing process is societal therapy: the whole of society is infected by the illness of torture, and punishment of the guilty constitutes a form of treatment. Professor Robert Daly, who treated victims of 'depth interrogation' in Belfast in the 1970s, believes that compensation is 'a first step in the process of rehabilitation. It allows the victim to take a less cynical view of the world, and to feel that justice has been done to him.' If torture aims to reduce people to silence, then the subject's return towards speech will make better progress if society recognises the facts and denounces those responsible. Hence the necessity, for the victims and their families and for society as a whole, that the events – torture or death camps – should be condemned and given a name. So it is that the tricks used to hide torture behind a clinical appearance and the lack of sanctions against torturers and their accomplices seem particularly unhelpful.

Social catharsis is a vital element in the medical cure. The Mothers of the Plaza de Mayo organise group therapy sessions where traumatic experiences can be talked over and shared, together with their struggle to have the crimes of the past recognised and condemned by society. Their work is an example to everyone concerned with fighting against torture and repairing the damage it does. No course of treatment can be undertaken without regard to the origin of the illness, if it wants to avoid trivialising events which cannot possibly be compared to the problems routinely dealt with by psychoanalysts. This is not to say that it is impossible to cope with distress, or to help the victims of repression to get beyond the 'unthinkableness' of what they or those close to them have been through. The one condition, as Maren and Marcello Vignar explain, is that the different levels of 'terror' must not be confused with each other: political terror, the total horror of torture, will always remain impossible to compare or reduce to the level of private terrors that date back to childhood.[9] 'They all suffered from a constant unease which poisoned their sleep and has no name. To define it as neurosis would be demeaning and ridiculous,' says Primo Levi about the survivors of Nazi extermination camps. Faced with these particular traumas, the therapist working with a tortured person cannot exercise his habitual 'neutrality' towards psychic disturbances. He cannot forget that in torture, unlike many ordinary traumatic situations, the victim had no option but to endure what happened to him. Only a firm denunciation of the torturer's madness may be able to liberate the tortured person from the guilt that haunts him, which is all too often fostered by society. But this 'real empathy that consists in accompanying the tortured person back into his history, is terrifying', says Dr Jean Claude Rolland.[10] 'Maybe it's the revelation of man's potential for inhumanity, maybe it's the dreadful, "diabolical" image of man presented by the torturer that we don't want to confront. But by doing that, we abandon the tortured person, who will once again be left alone and isolated to deal with what is revealed.'

International solidarity

Ever since the end of the Second World War, with the principles that resulted from the Nuremberg Tribunal, ethics have been an international concern. The Geneva Convention on armed conflicts,[11] several texts of the United Nations, the International Covenant on Civil and Political Rights, the Standard Minimum Rules for the Treatment of Prisoners – all these echo the concerns of medical ethics. Under pressure from medical professionals (doctors, nurses, psychiatrists and psychologists) and human rights groups, the UN Principles of Medical Ethics were adopted in 1982.

Human rights groups and medical bodies such as the Johannes-Wier Foundation and the International Commission of Health Professionals have forged links between different countries. The American Association for the Advancement of Science has sent missions to Uruguay, Chile, South Africa and the Philippines. Médecins du Monde sent a mission to the Soviet Union in 1988 to observe developments in psychiatry. Amnesty International has had medical groups since 1973, to support imprisoned doctors, intervene specifically on conditions experienced by prisoners of conscience and to mobilise the health professions in pursuit of its objectives. In 1981 Dr Alain Bernard, one of the founders of the French Medical Commission, went to Bolivia to examine Genaro Flores, an agricultural trade unionist who was in a critical condition in prison. Dr Bernard's intervention enabled Genaro Flores to be taken to France for treatment. In 1982 Danish experts went to Spain to investigate the death of Dr Esteban Muruetagoyena. Several medical missions sent by non-governmental or by professional organisations have also seen the light of day. Amnesty International has also encouraged the establishment of treatment centres for the victims of repression and exile. It has contributed to a string of international conferences: Athens in 1978, followed by

Geneva, London and Paris. In 1986 in Copenhagen, the Rehabilitation Centre for Torture Victims organised another international conference. Uruguayan and Chilean groups followed suit in Montevideo in 1987. Finally, in Paris in 1989, the French Medical Commission of Amnesty International organised the conference on 'Medicine at Risk – the doctor as abuser or victim' which marked a new stage in the development and co-ordination of international opposition to medical involvement in human rights violations.

8 Putting international standards to good use

'Even in prison, Dr Koryagin could feel the effects of international intervention through his torturers' changes in attitude,' says Dr Vianu.[1] 'When someone has taken the risk of speaking out, he must be supported.' In a psychiatric hospital in one of the most isolated countries in the world, with no chance of appealing to the law or a national code of conduct, or even to Soviet civilian society, Dr Koryagin's support came from abroad.

Since the end of the Second World War, committed citizens all over the world have provided a lifeline for dissidents who resist totalitarianism and despotism. The 'right to intervene' is a by-product of the UN Charter, based on the assertion of the universality of human rights, and it has been at the core of Amnesty International's action for nearly thirty years on behalf of prisoners of conscience and against torture and the death penalty. For the health care professions, an international code of conduct can take over where national codes and systems of justice are inadequate.

'Experimentation is prohibited in all cases where consent has not been obtained.' That is a clause from a circular issued by the Ministry of the Interior of the Third Reich. The attitude towards this rule in the death camps, with the direct or indirect complicity of a large section of the German medical profession, is a clear enough sign of the limitations of a code of conduct. The persistent use of torture in prisons in Turkey, a member of the Council of Europe and signatory to the European Convention for the Prevention of Torture, shows that the existence of international standards is not enough in itself to impose respect for fundamental rights. Individual and collective ethics and positive public action in support of human rights are the driving force in developing national and international codes and laws, and making them effective. Health professionals in the human rights movement need support, but in the majority of the countries concerned they come up against blockages at State or professional level.

Dr John Dawson, of the BMA, explains: 'There are two types of situation. In some countries, health care professionals and their organisations are in conflict with the government. It is then a case of helping them, from outside, to resist more effectively. In other countries, practitioners are isolated through the passivity or complicity of their own professional organisations.' 'Some of them don't denounce the violations they witness, because of their own political convictions,' says Dr Bénédicte Chanut, who was sent on a mission to South Africa by Médecins du Monde. 'But others don't do it because of the physical or moral pressures they are put under. In that case, the local Medical Association could play a very import-ant role, but the Medical Association doesn't intervene because it also has convictions that are close to the government line, so international pressure is crucial.'

The isolation of the doctor in resistance is generally in pro-portion to the seriousness of the violations. The situation in Chile is the exception that proves the rule, thanks to the remarkable stand taken by the influential and independent Colegio Médico which represents almost the whole of the profession. In Turkey, the majority medical association is also independent, and opposed to torture and the death penalty (see box on p. 89), but its scope is restricted by the fact that the government had the final say on the code of professional conduct prepared in 1989. In Pakistan and Algeria, as in South Africa, there is no professional authority at national level to support ethical awareness and intervene in basic medi-cal practice on the sole basis of a national ethical code. Even in the United Kingdom, preventing the use of torture took the concerted action of concerned professionals, the British and Irish Medical Associations, Amnesty International and the Council of Europe, as well as reference to the Tokyo Declaration. In the USA, the efforts of the medical profession, with worldwide backing, have not managed to reduce the involvement of doctors in the death penalty. Apart from an

Medical investigations in Turkey

In a letter to the Prime Minister, Mr Turgut Ozal, in July 1989, the Turkish Medical Association, the Ankara Association of Jurists, and a pharmacists' association asked for a 'Council of Doctors' to be set up to investigate allegations of torture at the request of prisoners' families or lawyers. They felt that an independent commission would represent a practical step towards the prevention of torture.

In June 1989, the Ankara section of the Medical Association had already suspended a woman prison doctor from practising for six months. The Association had proved that she filed a clinical report on a prisoner which omitted to mention any traces of ill-treatment. A second report by another doctor four days later did mention marks which showed the prisoner had been beaten up. The second report led to legal action against five police officers, and the doctor was also summoned to appear in court.

From the Turkish press, July 1989

optional European protocol, international law has not formally prohibited capital punishment, although on two occasions in the 1970s the UN General Assembly invited member nations to move towards abolition.

International law, an instrument which can be improved

During the 'Medicine at Risk' conference it became clear that international law and ethical rules are important but inadequate. In Pakistan, the Tokyo Declaration enables doctors to argue against involvement in corporal punishment. But their position is weakened by the failure of international law to provide explicit condemnation of this form of ill-treatment. To what extent could international law and codes of conduct, barely in their infancy, be developed into more effective instruments for doctors who resist torture?

International law makes scant reference to medical practice and human rights in peacetime. Article 7 of the International Covenant on Civil and Political Rights prohibits torture and medical experimentation without consent, but is the only international law in force that deals with medical practice. A committee that oversees the application of the Covenant can examine complaints and intervene with the States concerned. Other documents containing references to medical practice, the Standard Minimum Rules for the Treatment of Prisoners, and since 1982, the UN Principles of Medical Ethics, do not carry the same legal weight as the Covenant. There is no special committee to see that they are enforced, although the World Health Organisation is invited to disseminate them.

The Standard Minimum Rules for the Treatment of Prisoners can be ambiguous. If they are applied from a low profile, there is a risk that doctors will condone punishments such as isolation and deprivation of food. There are also gaps in the Principles of Medical Ethics. They allow medical assessment in the context of the death penalty, and the bar on doctors' being involved in 'cruel, inhuman or degrading treatment' is limited to forms of treatment denounced in the UN Convention against Torture, excluding capital and corporal punishment which are described as 'lawful'. The participants in the 'Medicine at Risk' conference, including those from countries where Islamic law is in force, were unanimous in their agreement that justifications of this kind are ethically unacceptable.

The right to 'intervene' introduced under international law is a difficult innovation for sovereign States to adjust to, and depends largely on pressure from individual citizens. States are not obliged by international pacts and conventions to account for their actions, unless they have ratified or acceded to them. Committees that supervise international pacts, even when they accept individual petitions, do not provide a genuine legal recourse in that they cannot judge individual cases. The Convention against Torture may assert the principle of individual responsibility beyond obedience to orders, but it does not have the means of enforcing it. The Nuremberg Tribunal was held in exceptional circumstances and does not constitute a genuine precedent. There is still no international tribunal to deal with crimes against humanity. Having been granted an amnesty in Argentina, Dr Bergès cannot have his case re-examined by an international court. He could, however, be tried in a country other than his own, under an interesting innovation of the UN Convention against Torture.

International law has been in existence for only forty years, and the gaps should be viewed realistically. The ambiguities concerning the death penalty and corporal punishments in the UN Principles of Medical Ethics are the result of long negotiations, and were the price to pay for an important step towards absolute condemnation of treatment that violates physical integrity. On the other hand, it is possible to rely on and encourage stricter interpretations of existing texts in order to contribute progressively to the strengthening of this new form of law. Several decisions by UN bodies and the European Court of Human Rights have condemned corporal punishment and thus given an example of a 'high-profile' interpretation of international agreements. The mobilisation of professional and non-governmental organisations contributes to this improvement. Given the medical profession's consensus on the principle of respect for life and physical integrity, it is easier to perfect the codes of conduct of worldwide associations than to change international law. Although governments write international law, it is also indirectly the result of citizens' efforts, and provides protection for individuals against the State.

The priority is to make international law work. The problem is how to make this international law a living force by involving the general public – and in particular non-governmental bodies – who would suggest new interpretations, draw up complementary codes of conduct and draw on concrete progress made in order to encourage further steps forward. By recognising the obligation to compensate and rehabilitate torture victims, the UN Convention against Torture has provided the basis for a grant to non-governmental treatment centres from the UN Voluntary Fund for Torture Victims. The European Convention for the Prevention of Torture has enabled a permanent prison visiting committee to operate in all the member countries of the Council of Europe. This committee can involve medical experts in its work.

The 'Medicine at Risk' conference made proposals to

increase the links between ethics and the law, and between professional associations and non-governmental and intergovernmental organisations. The principles of medical ethics agreed by all the European medical councils could be formalised in an additional protocol to the Convention on Human Rights. This would make the European Court more accessible to cases of violation of medical ethics.

There was a proposal to establish in the long term a 'Committee on Medical Freedom' within the World Health Organisation. On similar lines to the 'Committee on Trade Union Freedom' which operates in the International Labour Office, it could deal with requests and complaints, impose penalties, and intervene to protect individual doctors or associations. Dr Claire Ambroselli[2] proposed a study of possible links between national committees on ethics[3] and international jurisdictions (the European Court of Human Rights, or the Committee on Human Rights responsible for the application of the UN Covenant on Civil and Political Rights).

The conference also suggested supporting work on behalf of mental patients being done by the UN Sub-Commission for the Protection of Minorities. Finally, there were long discussions on the possibility of international protection for doctors or non-governmental organisations taking risks in repressive circumstances, either in their own country or abroad. In June 1988, at the request of medical aid organisations,[4] the Council of Europe drafted a set of principles of 'protection for humanitarian medical missions' for presentation to the United Nations in 1989. In December 1988 the UN General Assembly passed a resolution allowing foreign doctors to volunteer their services to countries where natural disasters occurred. The principle could be extended to cover armed conflicts. Many situations would still not be covered by a resolution of this sort, and nor would doctors belonging to the country concerned. Some of the conference delegates proposed an international status of neutrality for doctors, similar to the neutrality of judges, although they were fully aware of the unavoidable responsibility and risk involved whenever health professionals take a stand on matters of principle.

A more demanding code of conduct

International standards of professional conduct and ethics need themselves to be given life and to evolve. They could also be reinforced by mechanisms for their application and by concrete measures to be taken in the event of their violation. The conference also suggested that the codes of the major professional associations could be more precisely worded. The World Psychiatric Association, for example, could explicitly denounce the practice of sending people to mental hospital for political reasons, which it failed to do in the Hawaii Declaration. The conference also gave a great deal of attention to the problem of identifying risk factors. These are scarcely mentioned in the declarations of the World Medical Association, though more so by the International Council of Nurses.

If these principles could be put into practice, through pressure on national authorities and also on professional associations which show little concern for human rights, they would act as an important regulatory factor. The Medical Association of South Africa and the Soviet Association of Psychiatrists were debated at length by the Amnesty International conference. The former still belongs to the World Medical Association, a fact that prompted the British Medical Association to withdraw from it.[5] According to the South African doctors at the conference, who were members of NAMDA, the anti-apartheid medical association (see box on p. 94), a WMA mission to South Africa in 1988 not only supported MASA's interpretation of health and human issues but also isolated NAMDA still further by presenting it as an excessively partisan group. They were worried about NAMDA's lack of protection, since South Africa is effectively excluded from international law by having no seat at the United Nations. The Secretary-General of the WMA, Dr André Wynen, was present at the conference but did not comment on this point. He does feel, however, that the criticisms of MASA are unfounded, and that it is being condemned for its strategy of 'negotiation' with the ruling power, which in his view is more appropriate to the South African situation than the 'confrontational' strategy of the Chilean Colegio

Doctors against apartheid

During the course of my stay in Paris, I've been able to gather
that people know quite a bit about South Africa. Perhaps a
lot more than they know about other countries, even about
their own country. But in the process I've also found that
people know so little about my country. And often in this
polemics of apartheid people lose sight of the human factor.
It is not my intention to present to this forum the horrendous
examples of torture which I as a physician have personally
seen in my country. That would bring you to tears. In any
event I cannot do so, I cannot speak on detention in my
country, I cannot give you any statistics, because I would face
immediate persecution on return to South Africa. So I have,
then, decided to speak about what my organisation is doing.
It would be unfair to the health professionals with whom I
work in my country if I did not, however, place their work in
its context. South Africa is at this point in time under a state
of emergency, which has given the security forces incredible
power. We see increasingly a number of assassinations and
disappearances of people, especially over the last three years,
and there have been horrendous examples of torture which I
have personally witnessed. That then is the context in which
we find ourselves as health professionals attempting to uphold
an international code of ethics and human rights. NAMDA
is an explicitly anti-apartheid organisation and we do not
apologize to anybody for that. We have formed and are part
of a number of detainee clinics throughout the country.
Obviously enough these detainee clinics are under a very close
State surveillance. We are also involved in first aid programs,
because of a situation in many of South Africa's townships,
many people do not have access to hospitals because police
are stationed outside hospitals. We are also involved in
primary health care settings where the government has
attempted to remove people because of the colour of their
skin. But I wish to say to the European people in particular,
you have witnessed a most bitter struggle and you have been
part of a persecution yourselves not too long ago, not to allow
history to repeat itself on the southern continent of Africa.

A NAMDA doctor at the 'Medicine at Risk' conference

Médico. In any case, the lack of any mechanism for debating this type of case at WMA level is a serious disadvantage.

Health professionals of a country that violates human rights could be excluded from international professional bodies, but such a move risks isolating the country's doctors still further. This problem is the medical equivalent of economic sanctions against States violating human rights. There should be no question of shutting out the Soviet Psychiatric Association, which asked to be readmitted into the World Psychiatric Association in 1988, when various signs of improvement were apparent. But recent legislative changes still do not seem adequate, and according to some sources there may be some difficulties in putting them into practice.[6] However, the conference delegates thought it advisable to insist on definite guarantees, and not to give up any means of pressure available today which would become much less effective if the Soviet association were readmitted. Dr Vianu, voicing a point of view shared by most dissident specialists, stressed the importance of concrete guarantees of good intentions. The release of all psychiatric prisoners, and recognition by the authorities of past abuses, would be a symbol of their determination to break with their former practices. An open letter by Semyon Gluzman in *Le Monde*[7] expressed a similar view. After a mission to the USSR in July 1989, American experts also recommended reforms. Although the Soviet authorities disagreed with some points in the report, they described it as a 'valuable and useful document'.

'The nebula'

International law and universally-accepted principles of ethics can be powerful weapons as long as they are backed up by direct action from the medical community and the whole of society. Northern Ireland is an example of how a situation may be changed for the better by the united effort of these forces. The support given to NAMDA by the BMA, Médecins du Monde and the American Association for the Advancement of Science partly compensates for its lack of international protection. With support from the International

Federation of Human Rights and Amnesty International, Algerian doctors were able to hold a conference against torture in Algiers.

It is the intersection of various methods which proves to be the most efficacious way to progress. The Copenhagen, Montevideo and Paris conferences thus have tried progressively to achieve a consistent approach which uses both official or semi-official professional bodies as well as representatives of intergovernmental organisations, human rights defence groups, ethics committees, and grass-roots medical organisations. This informal support network now appears the most valuable instrument which should be developed and consolidated. The Montevideo conference on Physicians, Ethics and Torture, in December 1987, thus instructed Danish doctors to set up a committee to examine national situations, produce new rules and establish an international ethical tribunal. The conference in Paris in the same year on medical care for victims of torture suggested centralising all information on problems of medical ethics in repressive situations in order that individual missions and interventions, from whatever sources, should be as efficacious as possible. It also proposed the twinning of medical associations from different countries, and the publication of a list of bodies capable of intervening in problem areas. There may be another conference in 1992. The 'nebula'[8] lying outside the nature of specific group and level is formed with flexibility and contributes to the mobilisation of individuals and to the building up of international law.

9   Independence and responsibility

Following the Montevideo conference in 1987, a team of Danish doctors was instructed to give consideration to new standards and the setting up of an international ethical tribunal to rule on ethical matters. The team decided to concentrate on the involvement of doctors in routine police work in Denmark. It drew up recommendations for the revision of the Danish Code of Criminal Procedure, which would provide the basis of proposals at an international level. Far from being a return to a 'luxurious' view of human rights which ignored the most serious situations, these recommendations went back to the departure point of preventive regulation. 'Our job,' says Dr Nicole Léry, 'is not so much to punish as to establish regulations.' Uruguayan and Chilean doctors were the first to draw up a list of risk indicators, which was taken up and completed at the Paris conference (see Chapters 2 and 4). It was through an international exchange of views, when both extreme cases and daily routine were discussed, that was born and developed the idea of finding regulatory measures to stop the progressive deterioration in ethical standards which we have described earlier. The four key notions behind the resistance to such deterioration are independence from the authorities, openness towards society, protection of the rights of the individual in situations of constraint, and responsibility for one's own actions.

Medical confidentiality and independence

Whatever, in connection with my professional practice or not in connection with it, I see or hear, in the life of men, which

ought not to be spoken of abroad, I will not divulge, as reckoning
that all such should be kept secret (the Hippocratic Oath).

In the fifth century BC, developing medical practice was
already aware of the explosive nature of any information relating to a person's body, and the abuse of confidence represented by divulging it. In the late twentieth century, with
the constant refinement of physiological techniques allowing
more precise manipulation of the patient, and with medical
expertise being associated with judicial decisions, policies concerning prisons and other matters concerning society, the Hippocratic Oath is more relevant than ever. Breaches of medical
confidentiality indicate a decline in ethical standards. If a doctor is unable to see a prisoner alone, and if the patient knows
that anything he tells his doctor in confidence may be used
against him by the courts or his jailers (worse still, if he does
not know this), the doctor–patient relationship is distorted
from the outset, and diverted from its therapeutic function.

The principle has not survived the test of reality. In the
age of social security and vast institutional hospitals, medical
secrecy has often become 'a gigantic open secret', as Dr
Wynen says.[1] In States subject to the rule of law, there are
many areas besides forensic medicine where confidentiality
is breached, supposedly in the national interest. It can happen
during preliminary investigations into assault or homicide,
in the control of contagious diseases, or in the armed services,
where a simple administrative procedure is enough to breach
medical secrecy. It is easy to criticise the handbook for South
African nurses, which tells them to denounce their 'terrorist'
patients. It is more difficult for a junior doctor in an ordinary
hospital to react automatically by refusing to give information
to the police when they come and question him about a patient
in the emergency department, or for a doctor in a prison hospital to close the door of his consulting room to prison staff.
Dr Bernard Jomier[2] says:

> Everyone agrees on the principle. What really matters is knowing
> what instruments will enable the doctor to preserve confidentiality
> about his patients' health. We have a code of criminal procedure,
> a penal code, and a code of professional conduct, which protect

medical confidentiality perfectly, and case law has reinforced the principle. But confidentiality isn't respected in prisons, due to the conditions doctors work under.

In a paper sent to the French Inspectorate-General of Social Affairs in 1988, Dr Jomier and his colleague Dr Seyler made a harsh indictment of the failure to preserve medical confidentiality in Fresnes hospital and prison, and made a number of suggestions for doctors as well as for the prison administration. The administration was to ensure that the doctor could send a prisoner's medical file to the relevant department in a sealed envelope, and that prisoners and warders should not be directly involved in medical treatment or the storage of case records. Warders should be trained to respect confidentiality. The medical staff should take care never to include precise medical information in administrative documents, should refuse to give information to prison staff, while explaining their ethical reasons for this refusal, and as far as possible should not allow the presence during consultations of personnel not bound by medical confidentiality.

'A doctor employed directly by the prison authorities will have great difficulty in refusing to give them the information they ask for.' Dr Jomier's proposals, as he freely admits, can only be put into practice if doctors are granted independent status from the penal institutions in which they work. The problem of confidentiality is linked to the more fundamental question of medical independence. Dr Moncef Marzouki[3] tells us that prison doctors in Tunisia are greeted by the prisoners in the same way they greet their warders. In most countries, prison doctors are directly dependent on the prison or military authorities, and it is only the reference to medical ethics that provides an element of counterbalance: 'Early in my career as a prison physician, I realised that there was a conflict as to whether we were working for this autocratic institution or serving our patients,' says Dr Kim Thorburn.[4] In the Soviet Union, doctors take an oath of obedience to the State and the Party, and until recently psychiatric hospitals were run by civil servants from the Ministry of the Interior.[5] In the most commonplace situations, prison doctors' low salaries and lack of job security contribute to reducing their room for manoeuvre.

'People know perfectly well that there's a difference between a doctor who is paid by an institution and one who isn't, since the contract of employment implies that the doctor is subordinate to his employer in a number of ways,' says Dr Wynen. The UN Principles of Medical Ethics require doctors to give prisoners 'treatment of disease of the same quality and standard as is afforded to those who are not imprisoned or detained'. But, as Dr Maheu asks, 'Do we always treat our hospital and private patients the same way?' Institutional and financial constraints, the need to refer to a hierarchy, the resources at the doctors' disposal, and their own economic situation, are all amplified in a prison context. This is why the Paris conference published a recommendation that members of the medical and paramedical professions should have a status which does not depend on the detention centre where they practise, bringing their situation closer to that of doctors in the public health service. In France, the running of the Fresnes Prison Hospital has been transferred from the Ministry of Justice to the joint ministries of Justice and Health, a move Dr Jomier considers has led to many improvements. Even supposing this could happen everywhere, the reality of working conditions in prison should be borne in mind. The pressure exerted by these conditions can shackle a doctor's independence, whoever the employer is. It would seem desirable therefore to have procedures such as autopsy carried out by a doctor from outside the prison. As Dr Dawson says, 'It isn't enough just to ask the government for independence. It's an on-going battle.' The criterion of independence is relevant also as regards medical groups, colleges and organisations, and in general all that may constitute a relay outside the prison.

Subservience of professional bodies to government always leads to submission and inertia in the face of human rights violations. The banning or persecution of independent bodies, in Algeria (see box on p. 101), South Africa or Argentina, is a clear indication of what is at stake. International or national missions offer the advantage of an outside view which can help as a regulatory factor, assuming their members are genuinely independent and can collect information from sources other than the government.

From dependence to autonomy in Algeria

It is vital that the structures governing health care staff should be independent. The quality of the individual practitioner largely depends on the credibility of those structures. In some countries, this is a long-established fact. In others, economic, administrative and scientific dependence marks the beginning of a deterioration in ethical standards. It does not take long for individual dependence to take on the dimensions of a collective perversion. When there is no forum for discussion, and doctors feel helpless and isolated, they will be inclined to give up and compromise. In Algeria, until the tragedy of October 1988, the promotion of medical school graduates was of course bound by scientific criteria but also by membership of the Party, which determined one's place in the hierarchy. The medical profession was so severely discredited by its submission that during the October troubles many of the injured did not go to hospital. Some of them chose to die at home rather than risk being denounced by the doctors.

When I was a prisoner in El Haraj prison in 1987, I told the prison doctor about two inmates who were HIV-positive, so that precautions could be taken against contagion, since twenty prisoners used to shave with the same razor-blade. I was not able to get this request followed up before my release. At a more fundamental level, the Algiers School of Medicine, which used to hold a thoroughly honourable position in the Mediterranean Basin until the 1970s, has been going downhill since the Medical Union was brought to heel. There is no code of conduct any more. Medical ethics, and ethics in general, have crumbled away to an appalling degree.

Despite this disastrous situation, the medical community has managed to limit the anguish of the October '88 tragedy, thanks to a few doctors who refused to accept mediocrity as being inevitable, though at the price of their personal comfort or their liberty. Thanks to medical staff who refused to hand over injured people to the authorities, there were fewer deaths and fewer cases of torture. In the region I come from, Kabylia, the medical community decided to take control of its own affairs, outside the Party. A democratically-elected ethical council has been able to reinstate professional morals in a community where the number of beggars and thieves had increased. Brotherhood has become a reality in Kabylia. Our area has recorded the country's best results in the battle against tuberculosis, according even to official sources. We hold regular 'science days' which attract the vast majority of doctors in the region and from the rest of the country as well. Our rate of absenteeism is one of the lowest in the country. Yet we have no extra resources. The novelty is that both the doctor and the patient know they are respected, and safe from arbitrary actions. The personal relationship has been humanised.

We have had twelve court cases in eight months, nine of which arose out of a conflict with an authority.

Dr Said Sadi, a founder-member of the Algerian Human
Rights League, at the 'Medicine at Risk' conference

Breaking the silence

According to Dr Chanut:

Medical confidentiality is a double-edged weapon. It can provide protection, but it can also be a means of covering up torture. That is why Médecins du Monde proposed adding a clause to the Hippocratic Oath that would release doctors from medical confidentiality in order to denounce the violence they sometimes witness.

To any human rights supporter familiar with torture, the right to secrecy can ultimately be paradoxical, since all torture by definition begins with a person being shut away in solitary confinement. 'It has been conclusively proved that closed places have an influence on torture. In a prison, the doctor often finds himself cut off from the outside world, and even within his professional environment he may have huge difficulties,' says Dr Bernard Jomier. 'One can keep quiet, and one can speak out,' says Dr Aigues-Vives. 'A doctor should not be dominated by a hierarchical authority that would prevent him from divulging facts that were relevant to his patient's health, if that were in the patient's interest and with his consent.'

Safeguarding medical confidentiality is not an end in itself. It is only significant as a means of protecting the patient and his privacy, which is what the torturer tries to obliterate. Confidentiality is primarily a right of the patient, and should not be confused with an obligation to be discreet. Similarly, safeguarding the doctor's independence and his right to prescribe the treatment he considers appropriate should never be interpreted as a blank cheque giving him unlimited power over the patient. It is simply the basic condition of a trusting relationship that respects the patient's will. A prison doctor's opportunity to refer to an employer other than the prison administration is not a privilege, but a guarantee of greater democracy through separation of powers. Transparence *vis-à-vis* society, respect for the wishes of the patient and the establishment of a contractual relation between the doctor and the patient appear therefore to be indispensable adjuncts to and the ultimate objective of the doctor's freedom.

'If the most obvious effect of torture is reducing people to silence, then the most effective regulator is talking,' says Dr Nicole Léry. The replies to the Amnesty French Medical Commission's questionnaire on minor everyday abuses of power were almost unanimous on this point. To the question, 'Do you think it better to keep quiet rather than betray professional solidarity?', an overwhelming majority of 92 per cent said no. 'Silence leads to abuses,' was one comment. 'Systematising the idea of professional solidarity makes you more likely to risk condoning and perpetuating intolerable attitudes,' was another. Many of the health care workers who answered the questionnaire felt the priority was to talk to the people concerned and help them to 'progress': 58 per cent of paramedics and 38 per cent of doctors recommended talking over problems 'between colleagues'; 41 per cent of doctors would talk to the Medical Council. Other possibilities were a discussion group (26 per cent of doctors, 41 per cent of paramedics), or trade unions. While only 21 per cent of doctors felt there was a lack of opportunity to pose the problem of abuses, 58 per cent of paramedics thought there was.

'The wall of medical silence often seems very difficult to get over,' said one doctor, and many people answered, 'I don't know if I would be brave enough to speak out.' Prison walls can only add to these difficulties. 'We must be constantly alert to any measures that could open up the system,' says Dr Jomier. At present the opposite is true, and the duty of discretion is frequently the written or implicit rule in many of the world's prisons. In Britain, for instance, 'what you may see in prison is covered by the Official Secrets Act and should not be disclosed.'[6] Recourse to the judiciary is not always possible, and the system is cumbersome and hard to use. Many certificates dealing with ill-treatment, and many assessment reports written by administrative authorities, which have such functions, end up in desk drawers. Moreover, professional authorities, as we have seen, do not always fulfil the function one might wish. At every level it is once again a question of improving and revitalising those possible external means to which recourse can be had, and to create others: discussion and study centres, informal groups and associations, independent sources of assessment and finally, 'interventions' from abroad through the Press or international oranisations, all these represent possible solutions to the problem of the doctor's isolation. 'There is always a risk that the prison doctor will give in to the temptation to take the law into his own hands,' say four doctors from Lyons.[7] By asking for his work to be assessed by outside authorities, the doctor can avoid letting his ethical standards drop. In such circumstances his presence may thus help to make prison walls less impenetrable. Like the judas holes made in the doors of the interrogation rooms at Castlereagh, Northern Ireland, the doctor's presence represents the indispensable glance of the outside world into these closed surroundings.

Dialogue and contract

'It is wrong to say we are unable to communicate, for we always can. The refusal to communicate is a fault,' Primo Levi wrote, based on his experience of extermination camps.[8] The total prohibition on communication in concentration camps as also happens in torture can again be a guide to us. If the acceptance of what the victim says is part of the therapy for people who have been tortured, then the establishment of a dialogue with the prisoner, recognising him as an equal participant in this dialogue, with his own rights, would seem to be the best method of preventing any possible lowering of ethical standards in the practice of medicine in prisons. At the very least, the doctor should refuse to treat a patient who is hooded or blindfolded. The doctor should state his own identity, and know who the patient is. A much more common occurrence is for a prisoner to be punished for refusing treatment, and this is another risk indicator. Telling the patient honestly what is wrong with him, and discussing possible forms of treatment, can help to rescue medical practice from the punitive system. 'When a patient who can't choose his doctor refuses treatment, it poses a major ethical problem,' says Dr Espinoza:[9]

As a doctor, I see an antagonism between the repressive system and my own objectives in treating the patient. I don't have any solution to this, but I do still think it's better to stay within the machine, even if you feel its tearing holes in your white coat. You have to be there to say you should be able to make an individual health care contract with every patient, even in prison.

Dr Espinoza adds, however, 'When you're trying to be clearsighted about everyday reality in prison, you become acutely aware of the gap between the scale of needs and the means of responding to them. The theory of identical health care for all is a goal we haven't reached yet.' The idea of a health care contract is also more of an objective than an established fact, even in normal medical practice. 'Consent isn't always a sufficient guarantee of the ethical nature of an experiment,' says Dr Tomkiewicz. 'The relationship between the patient and the hospital,' says legal expert Dominique Thouvenin,[10] 'is by nature statutory, not contractual.' She therefore considers it impossible to talk about consent or negotiation of treatment in this context. The rights of a patient in prison are also problematic. The 'Medicine at Risk' conference decided to regard medical experimentation in prison as a risk factor, even if consent seems to be fully guaranteed. In the view of Dr Aigues-Vives, the broader concern is 'to think about protecting people who have no choice over their treatment, people whose state of health or handicap makes them isolated. They are still individuals with rights, and should get the benefit of help from outside the institution, such as the right to a second opinion, and visiting rights.'

Everyone is responsible

When doctors involved in torture or punitive practices are called before legal or ethical tribunals, they claim that they were not responsible. It was not their decision to torture or execute anyone, even when their medical report was used to condone the verdict or the practice. When they were present in a supervisory capacity, they were not responsible for the action itself. If treatment was given at the wrong time by the prison staff, the doctors were not responsible. The agent who carried out an order was not responsible, he was only doing as he was told. A person who has been 'conditioned' by his upbringing or by disturbances in early childhood cannot be held responsible, as Dr Lobo suggested. Arguments of this type have recently been supported by amnesty laws in Argentina and Uruguay, and by the attempts of the Uruguayan military hierarchy to shield army doctors from the ethical judgment of their peers, on the pretext that ethical codes do not apply in the army. This plea was widely invoked by Nazi war criminals, but rejected by the Nuremberg Tribunal. The principle of personal responsibility was stated by the Nuremberg court and has been taken up in various international texts. The United Nations Convention against Torture states: 'An order from a superior officer or a public authority may not be invoked as a justification of torture.'

Dilution of responsibility emerges therefore as a risk factor, like the absence of independence and of transparence. As Dr Marzouki says:

> It is essentially the power structure that prompts abdication of responsibility and minor acts of cowardice. In an authoritarian, pyramid-shaped structure, there is no retro-supervision or means

of evaluation, or openness. People submit to orders, they're reduced to the level of executive agents. They often end up by fitting into the system, and trampling on smaller fry. The only way to prevent these aberrations would be a circular structure with constant evaluation built in. And for us in Tunisia, the fight for human rights goes hand in hand with the fight for democracy, for the individual's right to self-accountability.

The 'Medicine at Risk' conference insisted strongly therefore on the responsibility of doctors. Whether they receive an unethical order, or give one without carrying it out personally, or prescribe treatment that is not properly applied, nothing can absolve them of responsibility. The same principle applies to nurses who are in the front line of day-to-day care and often have to carry out other people's careless orders. Among the replies to the Amnesty questionnaire, many nurses said they felt fully responsible for their actions but were worried about the difficulty of getting anyone to listen when they disagreed with things they were asked to do. The International Council of Nurses issued declarations in 1975 and 1983 stating nurses' professional responsibility in the care of prisoners and safeguarding human rights. Unfortunately this principle is often incompatible with national legislation and also with doctors' behaviour, which tends to reduce nurses to a purely executive role.

Ethics makes everyone responsible. As Dr Nicole Léry says, 'No law or code of conduct can solve all ethical problems, or analyse the details of every case.' 'People who take part in missions,' says Dr Dominique Martin, 'have a share of responsibility which they must accept right to the end.' No umbrella code of conduct can ever really protect people from taking risks. 'As a doctor,' says Dr Slobodan Lang,[11] 'I would regard it as unethical to ask for special protection.' Ethics, in Dr Benasayag's view, 'isn't just something we learn, that can protect us in advance from all the choices we have to make in life. In this area you never obey orders, even if they're good orders. Torturers are responsible, and some day they will have to face the consequences of their actions. But those who decide to resist are responsible, too.'

They may be responsible, but they are not alone. When

Dr Lobo's colleagues listened passively to what he told them, they took on their share of responsibility. The eradication of torture does not depend solely on the responsibility of doctors, or even public authorities. 'It must be said quite clearly,' Primo Levi wrote of the Nazi war criminals, 'that they were all responsible, to a greater or lesser degree. But it must be equally clear that behind them, there is the responsibility of the vast majority of the German people.' The experience of doctors who commit torture, as well as those who resist it, emphasises the importance of responsible citizenship in preventing violations of human rights.

10   Learning to say 'no'

How can people learn to resist and react to the gradual erosion of standards as well as to dramatic unexpected abuses? How can we ensure that the cries of 'never again' uttered throughout history after every catastrophe become more than wishful thinking? How can we convey something of the unspeakable experience of torture or concentration camps in a way which will make it impossible for such things to ever happen again anywhere? How can we educate people so that they will resist rather than collaborate and become involved in torture? These questions are as painfully relevant today as they were in the immediate aftermath of the collapse of the third Reich Nazi regime. It is in education, training and information that we find the main hope of tackling the real or feigned ignorance which allows these practices to continue. To inform, to bear witness, these are seen as absolutely basic duties by both survivors and those involved in human rights associations, for they provide a means of breaking the silence behind which torturers shelter. The hope that the message will finally be understood plays a crucial role in the struggle for human rights to be respected; one continues somehow to believe that education can, to use the terminology of the Universal Declaration of Human Rights of 1948. 'Education shall be directed to the full development of the human personality and to the strengthening of respect for human rights and fundamental freedoms.' Various international standards reflect this goal, for example the Convention against Torture:

> Each State Party shall ensure that education and information regarding the prohibition against torture are fully included in the training of law enforcement personnel, civil or military, medical personnel, public officials and other persons who may be involved in the custody, interrogation or treatment of any individual subjected to any form of arrest, detention or imprisonment.

Over the past few years, particularly in the area of medical ethics, initiatives have been taken in human rights education, although these are still in the early stages. In Denmark, the Netherlands and the United States, human rights are part of training courses for doctors, nurses and physiotherapists. In Chile, advertisements about doctors' involvement in torture have appeared in the newspapers and an on-the-job training scheme is offered by independent bodies. In France, various isolated experiments have taken place in medical faculties, and the inclusion of ethics in nurses' training allows for outside involvement in the course by organisations such as the Amnesty Medical Commission. More generally, school textbooks, visiting lectures by NGOs members in secondary schools, public discussions, and radio and television broadcasts all help to inform the public about human rights. Similarly, in the United States, general education in human rights takes place in high schools. In Tunisia, the Human Rights League has arranged for human rights teaching in schools to take place, and aims to revise school textbooks in collaboration with the Ministry of Education (see box). In Switzerland, debates are organised in schools and in community centres of all the religious denominations. Throughout the world, the day to day work of human rights activists is largely directed towards informing the public through the media in order to both educate and mobilise them, and to secure the active involvement of more people.

The roots of horror

I would like to give you a perspective on torture and other horrors, from a situation of conflict and crisis in a Third World country. Torture is a symptom of a deeper social malfunction, and treating the symptoms is not enough. In the villages where the Human Rights League goes to teach, we come up against three major problems. The first is poverty. In 1984 there was an extraordinary explosion in Tunisia which they called 'the bread revolt'. People went out and demonstrated in the streets, quite simply because they were hungry. The bread revolt led to all sorts of lapses on

the part of the people and the authorities. People were
tortured, and put to death. Poverty is the driving force behind
violations, and in the places we go to, people tell us, 'I need
water, I need a school. These are my rights.'

The second limiting factor is the State. In many Third
World countries, this almost means a state of nature, which
has not been domesticated by civilised society which is unable
to cope with economic and social problems. So in a way it's
the State that allows violence to go on rotting the social
framework.

The third and most recent obstacle is that we are seeing
now a generation of young people emerge who revert to the
oldest writings and most dogmatic interpretations of Islam.
As a Muslim, I am humiliated to hear Islam put on trial all
round the world because of the inhumane, reactionary use
it is being put to. Like all religions, Islam is very complex,
but its fundamental principle is humanism. As human rights
activists, we are caught in a dangerous dilemma, between the
risk of setting ourselves beyond the margin of society and the
risk of cutting ourselves off from a universal movement.

In the face of all these obstacles, and all these factors that
lead to torture, we have to keep telling ourselves that although
it's utterly foolish to want to change the world, it's even more
criminal not to try.

Dr Moncef Marzouki, President of the Tunisian Human
Rights League, at the 'Medicine at Risk' conference (summary)

The limitations of education

But how can we decide whether all these reports and education
schemes are really having the desired effect? When we believe
that we are educating the public, are we doing anything more
useful than providing them with information? In providing
this information, are we doing anything more than sending
out a message in a bottle, hoping it will reach its destination?
At the Paris conference, the members of the working group
on training, all of whom were directly involved in this area,

admitted they could not assess the effectiveness of their activities, apart from the fact of a general increase in public awareness. The question is how to find a message likely to help people not towards having an easy conscience because things are straightforward, but rather towards an awareness of risk situations which would enable them to say 'no' rather than 'I didn't know'.

'It has happened, so it can happen again: that is the nub of what we have to say,' wrote Primo Levi.[1] It happened, as he stressed, in Europe, in 'a civilised country which had just emerged from the cultural flowering of the Weimar Republic'. If Kant's moral philosophy in no way prevented the rise of Hitler and Dr Lobo's Freudian training[2] did not protect him at all from committing errors, just as his 'Pavlovian' counterparts in the USSR did, it is perhaps unrealistic to expect great things from the addition of a few courses in medical ethics to the undergraduate medical syllabus. Recurring human rights violations limit the extent to which we can trust in the influence of education. As both the scientific extermination practised by the Nazis and the medicalisation of torture show us, neither education nor culture, particularly if these are largely technological, are enough in themselves to guarantee that humankind will act more morally. The intrinsic value of technical progress is negated by the use of torture or execution. Far from showing us an image of humanity which is absolutely other, archaic or diabolical, the inhumanity of concentration camps and torture is only too human. This inhumanity is that of normal human beings made of 'the same stuff as ourselves',[3] and can be modernised like anything else. Moreover, both routine and more extreme examples show how easy it is to use medical diagnoses, as well as political or racial criteria, as an excuse to deny any human character to a patient. The debate surrounding the 'humanisation' of torture or the dilemma of a doctor confronted with a prolonged hunger strike bear witness to the complexity of ethical decisions.

Risk situations are characteristically in those 'grey areas' of ethics and human rights, where it is hard to distinguish what is humane from what is inhumane, and equally difficult to determine when standards are not being observed. In these areas of uncertainty, abstract knowledge and good intentions are not enough. Like a *kapo* or an ordinary citizen under a dictatorship, the doctor is, in some situations, caught between the Devil and the deep blue sea. Whether an abuse is minor or dramatic, a certain professional short-sightedness appears to be extremely widespread (see box). This is why health workers must be made aware of possible pitfalls, which may not be immediately obvious to a junior hospital doctor when the police demand confidential information, or when he is faced with State or institutional violence. 'In 1957 I examined a Moroccan woman who had marks of electric shock treatment on the vulva, and I filled in a certificate recording the fact. I blamed myself afterwards (being surprised and ignorant) for not having done more,' a doctor wrote in a letter to the French Medical Commission of Amnesty. In a routine situation, it is even harder to spot pitfalls. 'I am quite horrified to see nice young interns who freeze up completely when they're faced with a patient, because nobody has taken the time to think about teaching them how to deal with their emotions,' Dr Cohen, a lecturer at the University of Paris XII, explained.

If I had my time again

When he was a young prison doctor in Ceylon, Dr Abdul Hussain was instructed to examine a man who had been condemned to death, to confirm that he was fit to be executed. The day before the execution, Dr Hussain's examination revealed a physically healthy man but, like a caged animal, the prisoner paced the floor, bathed in sweat with rapid pulse and raised blood pressure. After the hanging, Dr Hussain had to certify that the man was dead, which took a long time to happen. According to an article in the *Journal of Clinical Psychiatry*, co-authored by himself,

Dr Hussain's role as medical officer, psychiatrist and medical examiner in these proceedings still troubles him greatly today. He feels a sense of guilt, and of outrage at having been used as a youthful, immature physician when he was emotionally and financially incapable of withstanding

what was demanded. He now vehemently avers he would go
to prison himself if faced with the same situation today rather
than so serve. Much as a soldier who has killed for his society
in a wrong war might feel, Dr Hussain feels a killer and
deplores his own weakness not to have acted otherwise.

From the *Journal of Clinical Psychiatry*, March 1978

Learning about the limitations

Simply teaching the theory of ethics cannot provide an
adequate response to dealing with these grey areas. However,
the very difficulties that arise in making ethical choices suggest
approaches to ethical education. An awareness of declining
standards can be developed by programmes which emphasise
the idea of limits and uncertainty. 'We should treat with
extreme caution the idea that an instrument could ever be
developed which would provide an answer to all our questions,
remove uncertainties and provide technical solutions to problems which are in fact philosophical, human and ethical,' says
Professor Lazarus. In 'risk zones' it is impossible to predict
every situation and find an answer to it in advance. As he
points out, over-precise definitions of what constitutes a violation in a sense justify situations just beyond the scope of the
definition: consider for example the definition of torture
simply as physical suffering or the concept of thresholds of
tolerance (six hours of forced standing). Ethical conduct cannot result from obedience to precise rules; such rigidity reflects
totalitarian conditioning and leads to causistry. Rather than
prescriptive teaching, general principles need to be tested in
practice.

These principles cannot be based on a strictly professional
approach. The limitations of technical knowledge must be
clearly defined to leave room for ethics. In certain complex
human and institutional situations, it is not technical knowledge which counts – dealing with old people who are bedridden or incontinent, invalids without social security cover,
or prisoners. There is in fact a risk that technical skill will
form a screen which makes it possible for philosophical or

political aspects of the case to be distorted or ignored. By apparently 'toning down' the harshness of punishments by medical skill in inflicting them, such punishments are legitimised; a supposedly objective view, unaware of its ideological foundations, can turn into a sophistry that justifies the most cruel treatments for someone labelled 'schizophrenic' or 'incurable'. An over-emphasis on technical skill can mean that treatment continues to be given against all odds. 'Doctors must be taught,' says Professor Tomkiewicz, 'that they can always treat an illness, but they can't always cure it.' Dr Sonia Jolles[4] says narrow professional training 'conditions us to keep at a distance from the patient'. 'Doctors, psychologists and nurses should be educated to recognise the limitations of their skill,' says Dr Benasayag. 'They should acknowledge that sometimes, when they have something to say, it is as citizens, not as technicians. Education about limits means education in ethics.'

Medical criteria, as we have seen, are necessary but inadequate as a gauge of practices. Respect for life, inscribed in traditional medical ethics, can be interpreted in various ways. In the modern version of medical ethics, which is slowly being worked out, the central idea is that of personal rights: the right to life and to medical treatment, but also the right to refuse treatment; the right to respect for one's body, decisions, and humanity; visiting rights; and the right of appeal against institutions. Doctors' and nurses' training should include teaching on the contractual and respectful relationship with the patient, who remains a human being and a legal entity, above and beyond his or her disabilities, his or her dependence and all medical or psychiatric criteria, not to mention those which are political or racial. The principle of professional responsibility for the patient, as stated by the Nuremberg Tribunal, is another important facet of this.

Doctors as citizens

To acknowledge the limits of a strictly professional approach is to recognise that society in general can be involved in medical questions and that medical ethics must take human rights into account. Simply stating what human rights are is not enough; to ensure respect for human rights, one must be aware of how this can be done and of the possible obstacles to their recognition. It isn't simply a diffuse knowledge of a general sort which is needed for abuses to be understood and combatted. The important thing is encountering the pitfalls in the course of daily reality. Applying constructive doubt, and evaluation with hindsight, can open up 'a re-evaluation that allows us to progress, as much as we can,' as Dr Emmanuel Maheu says.[5] Questioning can give a choice which cannot be guaranteed solely by technical or ethical knowledge. Medical training can anticipate this understanding with hindsight by opening up the debate surrounding 'decisional conflicts'.[6]

As we have seen, the obstacles stem from the very nature of medical practice and from the complex human problems which come into play in the doctor-patient relationship. As Dr Cohen explains:

> In his real-life work the doctor will be dealing with an uncontrollable element which he hasn't learnt about, and which can't be taught academically. A doctor's relationship isn't with parts of the body but with another human person, and the doctor's own reaction to that person will not be entirely predictable. If a patient refuses a certain form of treatment, or a woman bursts into tears in the surgery, the 'mechanism' breaks down. What's the doctor supposed to do?

With his clinical students in general medicine, Dr Cohen tries to adopt a collective approach to the difficulties of everyday practice. His concern is 'to create resistants, aware that we are human and we each have our own failings and background, to move beyond medical ideology and our own credulity, and to become critical of the standardisation that lies in wait for us.'

What should be done in the even more delicate situation of a prison revolt? Social, political and institutional factors also get in the way of an ethical practice of medicine. In ordinary medicine as well as in prison, economic considerations play a huge role in the right to treatment. There is a strong risk that dependency on political, judicial or prison authorities will lead him or her to forget the duty to respect the patient.

Dr Amar Jesani, who runs a community health centre in Bombay, has seen for himself doctors' lack of concern for the diseases arising from poverty and undernourishment. Dr Maheu reports that 25 per cent of the people who use the 'France quart monde' mission run by Médecins du Monde arrive there after having passed through the public system, and has also noted that many doctors switch off when it comes to social problems. Future health professionals should be given a basic education concerning the nature of a social group and the forms of discrimination and power mechanisms which can distort the doctor-patient relationship.

Just as they are largely ignorant of the indicators of risks, doctors do not always know about the resources available to combat abuses. 'People may let things happen because they're afraid to get involved, or because they simply don't know what to do or how to do it. They don't know where to turn to, or how they have more or less chance of asserting their point of view and staying alive,' Professor Lazarus explains.

A good many medical students aren't familiar with the basic principles of democracy, such as the separation of powers. They don't realise that if the same person drafts a rule, enforces it, and controls the way it's enforced, that confusion contradicts the foundation of the democratic state. This kind of ignorance leads to the reaction I once heard from a prison medical inspector when the administration asked him for explanations: 'Don't worry, I've inspected myself, and I made a good job of it!'

In order to combat abuses effectively, the future doctor must know about the various legislations he or she can make use of – legal tools such as national and international law as well as professional codes of conduct (see box).

Health, the fourth power

I have just told you about some recommendations on training, but if I was going to put them into practice in my capacity as a teacher, I would not take the decisions on my own. I would take them with other people representing my country, who could point out aspects of the medical power system in which I operate which I miss because of my own educational background. I happen to teach public health, which is a very difficult area. It means I also teach the way institutions and the State and the economy work, and also certain aspects of private life . . . And I notice that there is no separation of powers when it comes to health care. We distinguish between the executive, the legislative and the judiciary, but health is considered to belong everywhere. And that creates a major ethical dilemma. Should we favour the general interest, or the particular interest? Whether we are treating old people, or the handicapped, or drug abusers, or how to behave as an expert witness, this question arises.

Professor Antoine Lazarus; presentation to
the 'Medicine at Risk' conference (summary)

'Rather than societies of wise men, I plead for a society of citizens,' was Noël Mamère's[7] summing-up in the workshop on training at the 'Medicine at Risk' conference. Medical ethics emerged as a very particular expression of responsible citizenship, implying as it does an ability to evaluate one's actions with regard to both general principles and practical concerns. The conference participants felt that this civic and ethical training should not be prescriptive or purely professional. Conveying ethical attitudes is not achieved merely by reading what has been written on the subject; rather it involves more active steps. One cannot become a responsible citizen if one simply applies rules without thinking. The principle of separation of powers cannot be assimilated if only doctors are invited to evaluate medical practice. The participants at the Paris conference therefore considered that training in ethics should not be the job of specialist teachers but should result from a multi-disciplinary and communal initiative, in which the approaches of specialists and the general public could complement each other.

From information to involvement

In his first account of life in the Nazi concentration camps,[8] Primo Levi describes a recurring dream that he and his fellow-prisoners used to have: the prisoner would be reunited with his family and talking about what had happened to him, but nobody would listen. 'Why,' he wondered, 'was the pain of every passing day translated so consistently in our dreams into the scene of the story being told over and over again, and nobody listening?' In his later books he analysed the way in which reality for the survivors very often matched up to the dream. 'The extreme nature of Nazi murders endows them with a certain unreality,' says Dr Lifton.[9] Because they are beyond understanding, and present us with an unbearable picture of humanity, first-hand accounts of human rights violations are deeply disturbing. To make 'the others', that is the people who have not been through the experiences, understand, one must overcome not only the barrier of censorship, but also that of incomprehension or good conscience. It is the case that if a doctor faced with the physical or moral deterioration of his patient becomes hardened through oversensitivity,[10] how much more is it true that the reader, listener or viewer will display distancing mechanisms when confronted with pictures and reports. At worst, the account will inspire terror, as in the case of photographs of corpses in the Guatemalan press. In other cases, it may encourage voyeurism; an Amnesty International campaign about women and torture was presented by *Cosmopolitan* magazine in 1986 in a very ambiguous manner. More often, the relentless stream of horrific news on television inspires callousness and a feeling of helplessness.

The way in which violations are reported is thus also a delicate as well as a necessary task. No one is neutral when human rights are violated – neither the medical staff nor the journalist nor even the witness. The risk of trivialisation, disbelief, and of reducing human suffering to a spectacle, is constantly felt by human rights activists as they carry out their task of informing the public. The facts do not speak for themselves; journalists are well aware of the power of a caption under a 'shock' picture which could not convey a clear message on its own. One fact can mask another, and one event can distract attention from another. A spectacular depiction of torture can only show the most obvious aspects of it, those which have the least connection with the experience itself, and this can only reinforce the audience's sense of unreality and lack of involvement.

Journalists are another group restricted by both institutional mechanisms and financial and political constraints. They also run the risk of 'serving or suffering repression', as Noël Mamère points out. This is why Professor Lazarus insists that 'there is much work to be done in training journalists'. Journalists, like doctors, can be ambassadors for human rights. Just as communication provides an excellent control mechanism for medicine at risk, a conscientious news service can ensure a degree of openness in penal and medical institutions. Access to fully-rounded reporting, that is reporting which goes beyond a depiction of an event as distant and isolated in order both to place it within the broader context of human rights violations and to include the human aspect of events, provides weapons for the citizen with which to understand and fight against the appearance of abuses. 'In my work in connection with this conference,' says Antoine Spire,[11] 'I have tried to question the doctor as a citizen about what motivates him deep down, and to unsettle him slightly.' When it comes to human rights abuses, we are all responsible. We have a responsibility to stop the worst from happening, to foresee it: whether we foster blindness (lack of comprehension) and inaction to combat them, it is as responsible individuals that we do so. Denunciations of barbarity often sound naïve, but constant awareness of individual responsibility can give substance to them. The figure of the doctor is emblematic of the abuses which are always possible in an institution or a society and which everyone must denounce and stop. It is within the context of this kind of societal regulation of practices, that eyewitness reports will have the most impact, an impact much greater than that achieved by the use of simplified, emotive images: this is how we can go about building what Dr Umit Kartoglu[12] describes as 'a new culture of human rights'.

Notes

1 Putting a 'human' face on torture

1. Edward Heath.
2. See Appendix for the complete Declaration and all relevant ethic texts.
3. Amnesty International, *Torture in the Eighties*, AI Publications, London, 1984.
4. Until 1988, Spain allowed ten days of detention in police custody. It was always during this period that ill-treatment and torture would take place. A law was passed in May 1988 cutting the period to a maximum of five days.
5. Michel Foucault, *Surveiller et punir* (Surveillance and punishment), Gallimard, Paris, 1975.
6. Quoted by Foucault, op.cit. Chapter on 'La douceur des peines' (The mildness of punishments).
7. See Robert J. Lifton, *The Nazi Doctors – Medical Killing and the Psychology of Genocide*, Macmillan, 1986.
8. Max Lafont, *L'Extermination douce* (Gentle extermination), Éditions de l'Aresppi, Paris, 1987. 40,000 mental patients in France, i.e. half the psychiatric hospital population, simply died of hunger between 1941 and 1944. Even now, most doctors are unaware that this happened.
9. Quoted by Lifton, op.cit.
10. *Parilla*: electric wires applied to a prisoner tied to a metal mattress-grid. Literally means 'grill'. *Falaka*: beating on the soles of the feet; also known as *falanga*.
11. Psychiatrist and director of INSERM U69 (National Institute for Health and Medical Research, France).
12. See Chapter 3.
13. See Chapter 7.
14. See Chapter 7.

2 The vicious spiral, or the temptation to torture

1. *Your Neighbour's Son* was a film made by a Greek psychologist Mika Fatouros and a Danish doctor Gorm Wagner, based on an interview with a Greek ex-torturer, and reconstructed scenes from 'interrogators' training'.

2. *Jornal do Brasil,* 14 September 1986.
3. Dr Antoine Lazarus, Professor of Public Health at the Faculty of Medicine, North Paris, previously a prison doctor.
4. *Médicine à risques, des principes à la réalité vécue* (Medicine at risk, from principles to real life) Amnesty International, 1988.
5. M.G. Bloche, *Military Physicians: Cogs in a System of State Terror,* AAAS, Washington, 1987.
6. R.J. Lifton, *The Nazi Doctors,* Macmillan, 1986.
7. Insulting epithet used by the French about Algerian combatants in the Algerian War.
8. Miguel Benasayag, *Utopie et Liberté,* La Découverte, Paris, 1986.
9. *Droits de l'homme et contrainte de la personne* (Human rights and constraint of the person), *Acta medicinae legalis et socialis,* no. 115, compiled by Professor Jacques Védrinne and Dr Nicole Léry.
10. This questionnaire was sent by the French Medical Commission of Amnesty International to several thousand health professionals. There were only just over a hundred replies.
11. These examples were taken from replies to the questionnaire and are confirmed by many other oral accounts, books and articles.
12. Christiane Vollaire, nurse and philosopher, is a member of the Amnesty Medical Commission. She has published an article on this topic in *Agora* nos. 7–8 (October – November, 1988).
13. Professor Tomkiewicz is currently carrying out research on violence against children in medical institutions.
14. This expression was used by one of the former Nazi psychiatrists interviewed by R.J. Lifton, op.cit.
15. L. Lenoir, J.R. Lavoine, G. Ostapzeff, 'Le Marquage médical du corps, ou quand le médecin se fait stigmatiseur' (Medical marking of the body, or, when the doctor becomes a stigmatist), *Droits de l'homme et contrainte de la personne,* op.cit.
16. Ibid.
17. Dr Catherine Bernard, *Prise en charge des malades psychiatriques difficiles en France* (Responsibility for difficult psychiatric patients in France), thesis for the State Diploma in Public Health, 1983.
18. Christiane Vollaire's expression.

3 Forensic reports are never neutral

1. L. Lenoir, J.R. Lavoine, G. Ostapzeff, 'Le Marquage médical du corps … ' (Medical marking of the body), *Droits de l'homme et contrainte de la personne (Acta medicinae legalis et socialis,* no. 115).
2. 'Aptitude à la détention' (Fitness for detention), *Droits de l'homme et contrainte de la personne,* op.cit.
3. National Medical and Dental Association, see Chapter 7, p. 78.
4. From an article by Lisa Belkin in the *New York Times,* 10 June 1988.

5. 'Ni Crime ni délit, psychiatrie et justice' (Neither crime nor offence, psychiatry and justice), *Actes* no. 39, February 1983.
6. Marcel Lemonde, 'Le Fou, le coupable, le psychiatre et le juge' (The madman, the criminal, the psychiatrist and the judge), *Le Monde*, 13 May 1989.
7. Representative of Médecins sans Frontières at the Amnesty International conference.
8. Representative of the American Association for the Advancement of Science at the Amnesty International conference.
9. Lenoir, Lavoine, Ostapzeff, op.cit.
10. President of the Comisión nacional de Etica médica, Uruguay.
11. Adopted by the World Association of Psychiatry in 1977.
12. Dr Said Sadi is a psychiatrist and one of the founders of the Algerian Human Rights League.
13. P. Lamothe, 'Aptitude à l'isolement' (Fitness for solitary confinement), *Droits de l'homme et contrainte de la personne*, op.cit.

4 Prison doctors and hunger strikes

1. Head of Professional, Scientific and International Affairs Division of the British Medical Association.
2. S. Buffard, O. Barral, J.-P. Do and D. Gonin, 'Le Médecin en institution pénitentiaire' (The doctor in penal institutions), *Médecine et hygiène*, 42, 1198–200, 1984.
3. Report by Catherine Denis, based on an interview with Dr Espinoza, senior doctor at Fresnes Prison Hospital; published in *Tonus*, 7 June 1988.
4. G. Berro, M. de Pena, N. Ricciardi, G. Mesa and G. Alvarez Urquili (Montevideo and Santiago), 'Responsabilité des médecins devant la détention abusive' (Doctors' responsibility in cases of prison abuses), *Médecine et hygiène*, 46, 2257–8, 1988.
5. Medical Association of South Africa, see Chapter 7.
6. Miguel Benasayag, *Malgré tout. Contes à voix basse des prisons argentines* (In spite of all that. Whispered stories from Argentine prisons), Maspero, Paris, 1988.
7. 'Psychologist said to be architect of abuse', American Psychological Association, December 1984.
8. Irène Barki, *Pour ces Yeux-là* (For these eyes), La Découverte, Paris, 1988. Deliveries took place in filthy surroundings, on the ground, in cars, etc; the cord was hacked through and the placenta wrenched out with no consideration for the patient. The mother and baby were then left in the cold, and sometimes separated immediately . . .
9. S. Maltaverne, 'Psychotrope et détention' (Psychotropic drugs in prison), *Droits de l'homme et contrainte de la personne*, *Acta medicinae legalis et socialis*, no. 115.
10. Former doctor at Fresnes Prison Hospital.

11. B. Jomier, *Approche de la médecine en milieu carcéral* (Medical practice in a prison environment), Post graduate thesis in general medicine.
12. See M. Benasayag, *Utopie et liberté*, La Découverte, Paris, 1986.
13. Article 390 of the French Code of Criminal Procedure specifies that if a prisoner embarks on a prolonged hunger strike, he *may* be force-fed, but only as a result of a doctor's decision and under medical supervision, and if his life is at risk.
14. Maître Paley Vincent, *Grève de la faim et intervention du médecin* (The doctor's intervention in a hunger strike).
15. Presentation to the first World Congress on Prison Medicine, Dijon, 1978.
16. Professor of Neo-natal Medicine.
17. Association for Victims of Repression in Exile, a treatment centre that specialises in rehabilitating torture victims.
18. *The Doctor's Role in a Hunger Strike*, presentation to the 'Medicine at Risk' conference.

5 The death penalty and corporal punishment

1. A. Beichman, *La Première Exécution* (The first execution), quoted in 'Les Professionels de la santé et la peine de mort', Amnesty International, French Section, 89 CA 158.
2. Ibid.
3. Head of the journal *Agora Médecine éthique, société*.
4. See the Amnesty International report, *When the State kills. The death penalty versus human rights*, 1989.
5. The quotations that follow are from Maître Thierry Lévy's book, *L'Animal judiciaire, les écrits et la mort de Claude Buffet*, Grasset, Paris, 1975.
6. Author's italics.
7. According to the Reuter's release on 23 November 1983.
8. The death penalty is also used, including death by stoning.
9. Head of the psychiatric hospital in Nouakchott, Mauritania.
10. Founder of the Pakistani medical organisation Voice Against Torture.
11. See particularly Bruce Jackson and Diane Christian, *Death Row*, 1980 and Robert Johnson, *Condemned to Die: Life under Sentence of Death*, Elsevier, New York and Oxford, 1981.

6 Punitive psychiatry and 'clean' torture

1. This statement was presented to the meeting on 'Isolation and Torture' organised by the French Medical Commission of Amnesty International in Paris in January 1985. Natalia Gorbanevskaya announced to the meeting her intention of giving no further testimonies, so as not to have to relive the madness.

2. 'Psychotropic Drugs and Detention in Psychiatric Hospitals for Political Reasons', *Droits de l'homme et contrainte de la personne, Acta medicinae legalis et socialis*, no. 115.

3. Officially, this system was abolished by the law of March 1988, and the hospitals concerned passed from the control of the Ministry of the Interior to that of the Ministry of Health. But the new classification of 'ordinary', 'reinforced' or 'strict' surveillance seems to correspond to the former distinction between 'ordinary' and 'special' hospitals, with an intermediate regime for patients who have committed 'socially-dangerous acts' without violence. This formula suggests that non-violent dissidence might be concerned. Moreover, according to an article in the *Literaturnaya Gazeta* on 28 June 1989, a Ministry of Health circular issued shortly after the vote on this law would appear to reduce the promised improvements to nothing, mainly by allowing 'social misfits' to be sent to mental hospital. Twenty-six American experts published a report on a mission to the USSR on 13 July 1989 saying that people were still being put into mental hospitals because of their opinions.

4. Report of the American Association for the Advancement of Science, September, 1988.

5. Essentially, modifications of muscle tone and regulation of involuntary and automatic movements, causing abnormal movements of the face and body, and Parkinsonian symptoms.

6. There has never been any formal proof that an international training centre for torture exists, or that transfers or meetings of staff have taken place. It does seem probable, however, given the routine transfer of technology between police forces of friendly nations.

7. This classification results from a collation of various papers, mainly Nicole Léry's 'traitements inhumains, cruels, dégradants: des indicateurs de la pathologie d'Etat' in 'Santé et raison d'État' (Health and the interest of the State), *Agora*, nos 7–8 (October-November,1988).

8. Amnesty International, *Torture in the Eighties*, op. cit.

9. Scandinavian conference on torture, 6–7 October 1979. *The physical and psychological results of imprisonment and torture*, Report of proceedings.

10. Memorandum on the conditions of detention of persons presumed or found guilty of politically-motivated crimes in the Federal Republic of Germany, Amnesty International 1979.

11. See particularly the experiments of Dr John Lilly and Dr D.O. Hebb, quoted by Lauret and Lassierra, *La Torture propre* (Clean torture), Grasset, Paris, 1975. Some of these experiments may have helped the development of 'clean' torture.

12. *Confession véridique d'un terroriste albinos* (True confession of an Albino terrorist), Stock, Paris, 1984.

13. Eva Forest, writer and journalist, 'Ways of Resisting Torture', contribution to the Amnesty International medical conference, Athens, 1978.
14. Commission's decision on petitions nos. 7572/76, 7587/76 from Gudrun Ensslin, Andreas Baader and Jan Raspe.
15. *Le Matin de Paris*, 21 January 1989.
16. Member of the International Association against the Political Use of Psychiatry.
17. Maren and Marcello Vignar, *Exil et torture*, Denoël, Paris, 1989.
18. In *Chronique d'Amnesty International*, April 1985.
19. Interview with Miguel Benasayag, *Actes*, November 1984.
20. Quoted by Primo Levi, *Les Naufragés et les rescapés, quarante ans après Auschwitz* (The shipwrecked and the survivors, forty years after Auschwitz), Gallimard, Paris, 1989.
21. See, among others, Primo Levi, op.cit., chapter on 'Shame'.
22. Cf. 'La Victime de la torture et son bourreau' (The torture victim and his torturer), *Droits de l'homme et contrainte de la personne*, op.cit.

7 Medical ethics and resistance to torture

1. In *Le Monde*, 28 May 1987, referring to information of the League of Human Rights in Romania.
2. Published in the journal *Psychiatres* (French psychiatric review) no. 37, 1979/2, on the Honolulu congress.
3. Underground publication, usually in manuscript.
4. See Chapter 6, note 3.
5. See Chapter 1.
6. Dr Francisco Rivas Larrain, Secretary-General of the Colegio Médico in Chile.
7. Expression of Dr Adriaan Van Es, president of the Johannes-Wier Foundation for Health and Human Rights.
8. *International Newsletter on Treatment and Rehabilitation of Torture Victims*, RCT, Juliane Maries Vej 34, DK-2100, Copenhagen, Denmark.
9. This is a considerable simplification of the approach developed by these authors in *Exil et torture*, Denoël, Paris, 1989.
10. Dr Rolland treated Tito de Alençar, the Dominican friar who was tortured in Uruguay and committed suicide in 1974. See Chapter 6.
11. Drafted by the International Committee of the Red Cross.

8 Putting international standards to good use

1. Member of the International Association on the Political Use of Psychiatry.
2. Doctor and philosopher; member of the French Committee on Ethics. (See note 3 below.)

3. France is the only country to have this type of ethical authority at present. The National Committee on Ethics in the Life and Health Sciences is mainly composed of doctors and scientists, and its work does not come into the precise field we are concerned with here. It has, however, made a decision prohibiting biomedical and pharmacological tests on prisoners.
4. Aide Médicale Internationale, Médecins sans Frontières, Médecins du Monde, Fédération Internationale des Droits de l'Homme.
5. See also Chapter 7.
6. See Chapter 6, note 3.
7. *Le Monde*, 25 July 1989.
8. Expression of Dr Moncef Marzouki, President of the Tunisian Human Rights League.

9 Independence and responsibility

1. Secretary-General of the World Medical Association.
2. Formerly a doctor at the Fresnes Prison Hospital, see Chapter 4.
3. See Chapter 8, note 8.
4. Dr Thorburn is currently Medical Director of Prisons in the State of Hawaii.
5. In principle, this situation was abolished by the law of March 1988, but, in fact, according to Mr Podrabinek, it still exists. See also Chapter 6, note 3.
6. Official Secrets Act. The quotation comes from Dr John Dawson, British Medical Association.
7. S. Buffard, O. Barral, J.-P. Do, and D. Gonin, 'Le Médecin en institution pénitentiaire' (The doctor in penal institutions), *Médecine et hygiène*, 42, 1198–200, 1984.
8. Primo Levi, *Les Naufragés et les rescapés, quarante ans après Auschwitz* (The shipwrecked and the survivors), Gallimard, Paris, 1989.
9. See Chapter 4, note 3.
10. Dominique Thouvenin, 'La Référence au contrat de soins dans les expérimentations sur l'homme', *Ethique médicale et droits de l'homme, la fabrique du corps humain* (Reference to a contract of treatment in medical experiments on human beings; in *Medical Ethics and Human Rights – the human body*), Actes-Sud/INSERM, 1988.
11. Professor of Public Health in Zagreb, Yugoslavia.

10 Learning to say 'no'

1. Primo Levi, *Les Naufragés et les rescapés* ... (The shipwrecked and the survivors), Gallimard, Paris, 1989.
2. See Chapter 2.
3. Primo Levi, op.cit.
4. Member of the French Medical Commission, and one of the producers of the journal *Agora*.

5. See Chapter 5, note 3.

6. Dr Cohen's expression.

7. Television reporter for the French television channel *Antenne 2* who presents the programme 'Resistance', on human rights.

8. Primo Levi, *If this is a Man*, Penguin, Harmondsworth, 1979.

9. R.J. Lifton, *The Nazi Doctors*, Macmillan, 1986.

10. See Professor Lazarus's analysis in Chapter 2.

11. TV reporter with France-Culture, particularly the programme 'Voix du Silence'.

12. Turkish Medical Association. See Chapter 1.

Appendix
Conference on 'Medicine at Risk: the health professional as abuser or victim'

(19, 20 and 21 January 1989 at UNESCO, Paris)
PART ONE: Participants
Guests

Dr Said Sadi – Algeria

Dr Said Sadi is a psychiatrist and was one of the founding members of the Algerian League of Human Rights (Ligue algérienne des droits de l'homme) which was established in June 1985. Shortly after its foundation, several of its members, including Dr Sadi, were arrested and imprisoned. He was sentenced to three years' imprisonment on charges of membership of an unauthorised organisation, distribution of leaflets and participation in illegal gatherings. Dr Sadi was imprisoned between August 1985, two months after the foundation of the Ligue, and April 1987, when he was released after serving a year and a half of his sentence.

Dr Ramiro Olivares – Chile

Dr Ramiro Olivares works with the Vicaría de la Solidaridad, the human rights body of the Catholic church in Chile. He was arrested in May 1987 and imprisoned after a man for whom the Vicaría had arranged treatment of a bullet wound was arrested for a violent crime. Charges were brought against Dr Olivares under the anti-terrorist law; others, including a lawyer from the Vicaría and doctors from the clinic where the man was treated, were similarly charged. These arrests were seen by many as an attempt to discredit the Vicaría, which is one of the largest human rights organisations in the country. Dr Olivares was released on bail in August 1987.

Dr Francisco Rivas Larrain – Chile

Secretary-General of the Chilean Medical Association (Colegio médico de Chile). The Colegio médico has over the last few years been particularly vocal in pressing for the observance by doctors of medical ethical standards and has held disciplinary hearings into cases of doctors' alleged complicity in torture. It incorporated very explicit articles into its ethical code to cover the role of the doctor if encountering torture, and in November 1985 held a colloquium in Santiago entitled 'The Role of Medical Associations in the Defence of Human Rights' to which other medical associations were invited. Among other steps taken by the Colegio were the publication of the Declaration of Tokyo in a daily newspaper, a public declaration condemning torture and calling for a closure of secret police detention centres. Dr Rivas was imprisoned in July 1986 together with the Colegio's president, Dr Juan Gonzalez, after a body known as the National Civil Assembly, of which Dr Gonzalez was named president, had called a two-day protest to call for a restoration of the respect for human rights. They were charged under the Law of National Security and held in prison until their release on bail in August 1986. They were acquitted in January 1987.

Dr Salem Negm and Dr Essam Al Erian – Egypt

Members of the Egyptian Medical Association, of which Dr Salem Negm is the Secretary-General. The Egyptian Medical Association, which numbers some 90,000 doctors, has made known its condemnation of torture and has recently carried articles on torture in the Association's journal. In addition, in mid-1987 they requested permission to visit prisons to inspect the health of detainees, but such permission was refused.

Dr Amar Jesani – India

Senior research officer at the Foundation for Research in Community Health, currently engaged in research into social aspects of medicine. Founder member and working editor of the *Radical Journal of Health*, Dr Jesani has published literature primarily on rural health care and the provision of primary health care in India. In the course of his work at the Foundation, he has documented information on instances of torture, and on the treatment and provision of medical care to prisoners in India.

Dr Alhousseyn Dia – Mauritania

Dr Alhousseyn Dia is Director of the Nouakchott psychiatric hospital. He was formerly President of the Mauritanian Association of Doctors, Pharmacists and Dentists at a time when judicial amputations were introduced in Mauritiania following the establishment of a court of Shari'a Law in 1980. The first amputations in September that year were reported to have been carried out by individuals with medical training, leading to strong protest from the medical association and the refusal of doctors to participate.

Dr Mahboob Mehdi – Pakistan

Dr Mahboob Mehdi is the founder of an organisation known as 'Voice against Torture' in Islamabad. The organisation aims to campaign publicly against torture and promote ethical awareness among physicians in an attempt to eradicate abuses such as spurious death certificates, failure to report torture, involvement in torture, etc. It hopes to work with the Pakistan Medical and Dental Council to incorporate relevant articles into the country's ethical code and aims to provide medical care for victims of torture.

Dr X and Dr Y – South Africa

Both are members of NAMDA (National Medical and Dental Association) created in 1982 after the failure of the investigations by the Medical Association of South Africa (MASA) of Steve Biko's physicians; NAMDA is an anti-apartheid organisation with about 3,000 members. The organisation's goals are:

- the medical follow-up of the victims of apartheid (participation in the activities of health-care facilities in townships and homelands, medical follow-up of detainees after their release from prison);
- the denunciation of inequalities in the health-care system;
- the planning of an alternative health-care system for the South Africa of tomorrow.

Professor Isam Ahmed – Sudan

Professor Ahmed is a mathematician at the University of Gezira in Wadi Medani. He was imprisoned from mid-1984 to December of that year for criticism of the Sudanese Vice-President. He was a member of the Republican Brotherhood, Islamic organisation, several of whose members were imprisoned on the same charges. His imprisonment followed the introduction of new laws based on Islamic Shari'a law which included the penalty of amputation for theft. Between the introduction of the punishment in September 1983 and the fall of President Nimeiri's government in April 1985, over 120 sentences of amputation were carried out, including both amputation of the right hand and 'cross-limb' amputation (amputation of the right hand and left foot). Since 1985 no amputations have been carried out, although some new sentences have been passed and over fifty sentences are currently outstanding.

Dr Moncef Marzouki – Tunisia

Dr Marzouki, professor of public health, is a lecturer at the school of medicine in Sousse and President of the *Ligue tunisienne des droits de l'homme*. (Tunisian League of Human Rights). He was formerly president of its office in Sousse. The *Ligue* was one of the first to be created in Africa; it was initially founded in 1977 and held its first national congress in 1982. Dr Marzouki has published on civil liberties and human rights. He has been active in calling for an end to the death penalty in Tunisia and, on behalf of the *Ligue*, has spoken publicly in recent months for its abolition.

Dr Umit Kartoglu – Turkey

Member of the Executive Council of the Turkish Medical Association. Dr Kartoglu is also a member of its human rights division. The Turkish Medical Association has taken a number of steps against human rights abuses. In October 1985 they submitted a letter to the authorities calling for an end to the death penalty; this led to charges being brought against six members of the Central Council under the Law on Associations which prohibits any political statements from associations. After a long trial, all were acquitted in September 1986. In late 1986, the Association drafted a revised code of medical ethics which includes clear guidelines on the doctor's duty with regard to the death penalty, torture and the treatment of detainees. The code has yet to gain legal approval. The Association receives many complaints from prisons and takes steps to ensure that their doctors are aware of and avoid human rights abuses. Their professional journal has carried a number of articles dealing with human rights, torture and prison conditions.

Dr Francisco Ottonelli – Uruguay

Dr Ottonelli is a lawyer who is President of the Comisión Nacional de Etica Médica (National Commission of Medical Ethics), a body created in July 1984 and comprised of doctors and laywers. The Commission was created at the 7th National Medical Convention, which was the first nationwide medical assembly to be held since before the imposition of military rule when assemblies were forbidden. The Commission was created to hear complaints against prison doctors which at the time were being brought by ex-detainees lodging complaints of torture. The Uruguayan Medical Association has encountered difficulties recently in their pursuit of action against military doctors.

Tamara Grigoriants – USSR

Tamara Grigoriants was born in Vladivostok in 1943. She studied foreign literature and journalism at Moscow University. From 1969 to 1975, she organised several international exhibitions. In 1975, when her husband, Sergei Grigoriants, was arrested for the first time, she was asked to resign. Some years later, she became editor of the journal for the Institute of Labor, where she worked until December 1988. She has worked since this date for the publication *Glasnost*. Her husband was adopted by the French Section of Amnesty International after his arrest in February 1983. He was released in February 1987.

Professor Slobodan Lang – Yugoslavia

Professor Lang is a professor of medicine at the School of Public Health in Zagreb, and organises regular meetings on human rights and medicine. One-week courses are held at the inter-university centre in Dubrovnik and are sponsored by universities from all over the world.

List of participants

1 *Non-governmental or intergovernmental organisations*

Dr Robert Kirschner and Janet Gruschow, American Association for the Advancement of Science, USA.
Dr John Dawson, British Medical Association, GB.

Dr Hernan Reyes, Head of the Medical Division, International Committee of the Red Cross, Switzerland.

Dr Adriaan Van Es, Vice-President, and Charles Graves, Executive Director, International Commission of Health Professionals for Health and Human Rights (CINPROS), Switzerland.

Dr Jorgen L. Thomsen, Committee of Concerned Forensic Scientists, Denmark.

Carol Corillon, Director, Committee on Health and Human Rights, Institute of Medicine; Committee on Human Rights, National Academy of Sciences, USA.

Peter Leuprecht, Council of Europe, Human Rights Division, France.

Lone Jacobsen, Senior Nurse, Danish Nurses' Organisation, Rehabilitation and Research Centre for Torture Victims, Denmark.

Dr Vianu, International Association on the Political Use of Psychiatry (IAPUP), Switzerland.

Miss J. Petrequin, International Council of Nurses (ICN), Switzerland.

Mrs Marion Rustad, Northern Nurses' Federation, Norway.

Mrs Tordis Flatas, Norwegian Nurses' Association, Norway.

Dr Peter Vesti, psychiatrist, head of department, and Dr Ole Vedel Rasmussen, International Rehabilitation and Research Centre for Torture Victims (RCT), Denmark.

Dr André Wynen, Secretary-General, World Medical Association, Belgium.

2   *French associations and organisations*

Dr P. Galimard, Dr Josette Vaquier, Medical Group of ACAT (Association of Christians for the Abolition of Torture).

Dr François Prévoteau, Dr. E Maheu, Agora.

Dr Christos Chouaid, former President, Aide Médicale Internationale (AMI).

Dr Hélène Jaffé, President, AVRE: Association for the Victims of Repression in Exile.

Dr Patrick Aeberhard, President, Dr Bénédicte Chanut, Dr Isabelle Marin, Médecins du Monde (MDM).

Dr Rony Brauman, Président, Dr Dominique Martin, Dr Jean-Luc Nahel, Médecins sans Frontières (MSF).

Fabienne Rousso-Lenoir, assistant secretary-general, International Federation of Human Rights (FIDH).

Dr Louis René, President, Dr Jacques Weil, Vice-President and President of the Ethical Council, French National Medical Council.

Marie-Claude Dayde, Secretary-General, National Union of Liberal Nurses.

3 *Amnesty International Medical Groups*

Dr Carlo Blondé, Flemish Belgium.
Dr Francine Quinchon, French-speaking Belgium.
Henrik Marcussen, Uni Lise Wissing, Joergen Kelstrup, Denmark.
Matti Wallin, Finland.
Dr Ase Berg, Norway.
Dr Evert Doornenbal, Psychiatric Committee, the Netherlands.
Dr Paul Lips, Dr Annemarie Raat, the Netherlands.
Charlotte Uggla, President, Sweden.
Nicole Cretton, Dr Claudine Jeannet, Dominique Turcas-Lorzier, Health professionals' group, Switzerland.

4 *Individual participants*

Dr Miguel Benasayag, psychoanalyst, France.
Dr Abram Cohen, psychiatrist, France.
Dr Espinoza, senior doctor at the Fresnes Prison Hospital, France.
Dr Bernard Jomier, France.
Dr Jacques Laurans, psychiatrist at the Fresnes Hospital, France.
Dr Nicole Léry, forensic doctor at Claude Bernard University, Lyon, France.
Professor Antoine Lazarus, Professor of Public Health, Paris-Nord Faculty of Medicine, France.
Noël Mamère, journalist, France.
Valérie Marange, journalist, France.
Antoine Spire, journalist, France.
Philippe Texier, President of the county court at Évry and member of the administrative council of France-Terre d'asile, France.
Dr Kim Marie Thorburn, prison doctor, United States.
Dr S. Tomkiewicz, psychiatrist at the National Institute for Health and Medical Research (INSERM), France.
Professor Jacques Védrinne, Professor of Forensic Medicine, France.

5 *Amnesty International*

International Secretariat:
Marguerite Garling, Research Department.
Gaëtan Mootoo, research assistant.
Nigel Rodley, Legal adviser.
James Welsh, Medical co-ordinator.
Janice Selkirk, assistant medical co-ordinator.

Amnesty International, French Section:
Carole Bat, Director.
Antoine Bernard, jurist.
Chantal de Casabianca, press officer.
Jacqueline Follana, jurist.
Simon Foreman, lawyer.
Aimé Léaud, jurist, former President of the French Section.
Marie-Odile Maurize, in charge of the Legal Committee.
Marc de Montalembert, President of the French Section until May 1989.
Wladimir Vinaver, International Commission.

Medical Commission:
Dr Claude Aigues-Vives, paediatric psychiatrist.
Liliane Bernard, in charge of the Medical Commission.
Marie-Hélène Beaujolin, psychologist and psychoanalyst.
Dr Patrick Cazalot, psychiatrist.
Dr Jean-Pierre Dejonghe, psychiatrist.
Sylvia Desmontaigne, member of the Amnesty Executive Office until May 1989.
Yvonne Deverly.
Claude Duhamel, psychologist.
Dr Robert Gautier, surgeon.
Dr Janine Glogowska.
Reine Goullin, psychologist and prison visitor.
Dr Suzanne Hugon, anaesthetist.
Dr Édouard Jean-Baptiste.
Dr Sonia Jolles.
Dr Dominique Kerouedan.
Dominique Lassard, nurse.
Dr Annette Lécine, radiologist.
Gabrièle Milot, nurse.
Line Pedoussat, teacher of nurses.

Dr Michèle Quazza, anaesthetist.
Françoise Sironi, psychologist.
Françoise Tagand, biology teacher.
Hélène Timsit.
Christiane Vollaire, nurse.

Notes on organisations represented at the Conference

French organisations

Aide médicale internationale (AMI). Founded in 1979, non-governmental, apolitical, offshoot of 'Médecins sans Frontières'. Its members are predominantly doctors, nurses and physiotherapists acting in a voluntary capacity to provide on-the-spot help for civilian populations in wartime, or minorities in cases of armed conflict, and training for health care workers. Its missions are usually clandestine, to reach populations who have no national health service (Surinam, Afghanistan, Burma, Colombia, South Sudan). Has a modest head office in Paris, the majority of donations being used to support missions.

Association pour les victimes de la repression en exil (AVRE). Set up with Amnesty International support in 1984. This is a treatment centre for torture victims staffed by a team of GPs and specialists, psychiatrists, psychologists, and social workers, some paid and some volunteers. It carries out medical missions abroad and makes information on torture and health available to the health care professionals and to the public.

Médecins du Monde (MDM). Non-governmental organisation founded in 1979 as an offshoot of 'Médecins sans Frontières': 'it provides volunteer medical help to populations hit by natural disaster, armed conflict or unusually difficult living conditions'. Its aim is 'to intervene wherever war, illness, famine or poverty constitute a threat to human life'. MDM is apolitical and works regardless of race, ethnic origin or religion (e.g. Afghanistan, the China Sea, the Boat People, Brazil, Chile, South Africa). Is also involved with people who do not qualify for Social Security in France, through the 'France-Quart monde' mission.

Médecins sans Frontières (MSF). Non-governmental organisation founded in 1969 by a team of French doctors to help the population of Biafra. Since then, MSF has sent emergency and development missions to many countries, staffed by medical professionals whose expenses are paid in the field (Central and South America, Africa, Central and South East Asia). Also involved in natural disaster relief.

Organisations from other countries

American Association for the Advancement of Science (AAAS). AAAS Committee on Scientific Freedom and Responsibility. The AAAS, based in Washington, is the umbrella organisation for US scientific organisations, grouping together several hundred such organisations. It established the Committee on Scientific Freedom and Responsibility in 1976 which publishes a quarterly bulletin entitled *Report on Science and Human Rights*. The Committee has sponsored investigative missions into human rights and published reports on scientists, engineers and health professionals who have suffered human rights violations or have had their freedom curtailed in their field of research.

International Commission of Health Professionals and Human Rights (CINPROS/ICHP). Officially established in January 1985 with headquarters in Geneva and national affiliated groups. Objectives include promoting human rights and the right to health for all, supporting health professionals who are working to safeguard human rights, and co-operating with NGOs and IGOs pursuing similar objectives. The ICHP publishes a periodic bulletin and has sponsored symposia.

Committee of Concerned Forensic Scientists. Resulted from an international meeting on forensic medicine held in Oxford in 1984 which discussed problems of forensic medicine and human rights. The secretariat is based in Denmark and the members are forensic specialists from all over the world.

National Academy of Science (NAS)/*Institute of Medicine: Committee on Human Rights*. The Committee on Human Rights of the US NAS was set up in 1976 to investigate and act against individual cases of the repression of scientists and scientific research. It was later joined by the US National Academy of Engineering and the

Institute of Medicine and is now active in cases of repression against scientists, health professionals and engineers.

International Association on the Political Use of Psychiatry (IAPUP). An international association of national groups active on the political use of psychiatry. Publishes a periodic information bulletin detailing individual cases investigated by the organisation, including all relevant information from countries where the political abuse of psychiatry has been documented, and information on professional meetings.

Johannes Wier Foundation for Health and Human Rights. Set up in 1986 in the Netherlands by a group of doctors, nurses, dentists and members of paramedical professions who saw the need in the Netherlands for an organisation concerned with human rights. Acts on cases of health workers who suffer human rights violations or become involved in them; provides information on human rights violations in the health field, promotes investigative missions and collaborates with other organisations engaged in similar work.

Northern Nurses' Federation. Confederation of Scandinavian Nursing Associations.

International Rehabilitation and Research Centre for Torture Victims (RCT). Established in 1982, RCT provides medical, psychological, social and legal support to torture victims and their families exiled in Denmark. RCT works in conjunction with Copenhagen's main hospital. Most patients are out-patients and receive three or four months' intensive treatment, plus after-care. The Centre carries out research into torture, runs a documentation service, and maintains contacts with other centres and interested individuals internationally.

British Medical Association (BMA) represented by Dr John Dawson, head of the Professional, Scientific and International Affairs Division of the BMA. He was a member of the Association's working party on doctors and torture, which resulted in the publication of the BMA *Report on Torture* in 1986. Dr Dawson is co-author of *Doctors' Dilemmas: Medical Ethics and Contemporary Science*, Brighton Harvester Press, 1985.

PART TWO: Conference recommendations

Working Group 1

Suggested agenda items:
- a clear universal definition of international principles of medical ethics;
- the scope and limitations of ethical principles as currently defined;
- ways in which to remedy ambiguities and omissions in the codes.

Recommendations

1 Medical ethical principles require that members of the health professions must refrain from any act undertaken without clinical justification which in any way threatens the physical and psychological integrity of any individual. For this reason we urge that national and international medical associations and human rights organisations support medical professionals, particularly doctors, who refuse to participate in executions or corporal punishment handed down under national penal law.

2 A doctor must not treat or intern an individual in a psychiatric hospital solely for his or her political or religious beliefs or for any reason of discrimination.

3 The working group:
   - reaffirms its commitment to Article 5 of the Declaration of Tokyo relative to force-feeding of hunger strikers;
   - affirms that no authority can force a doctor to order or implement the force-feeding of a hunger striker;
   - calls upon international medical organisations to support doctors who refuse to cooperate in force-feeding.

4 Associations of health professionals should work towards achieving the independence of members of the medical and paramedical professions from the administrative authority of the places of detention in which they practice.

Working Group 2

Suggested agenda items:
- what international remedies are there for risks to the ethical practice of medicine?

- ' how can transnational interventions be arranged?
- how can existing international mechanisms be improved?

Recommendations
1 The working group recommends that, as provided for by the European Convention for the Prevention of Torture, visits by independent international bodies to persons deprived of freedom be instituted universally and that these visits take place at any time and to any detention centre.

2 The working group recommends that sanctions should be taken against anyone, including doctors, having participated in acts of torture, torture being recognised as a crime under international law and subject to international jurisdiction. Doctors found guilty of participating in acts of torture should be expelled from their professional organisations and prevented from practising medicine, even outside their own country.

3 The working group supports the draft report of the Sub-commission of the UN Human Rights Commission relative to the treatment of the mentally ill.

4 The working group recommends the creation of committees of Freedom in Medicine within various IGOs, notably the World Health Organisation (WHO), and that medical NGOs be represented within such committees.

5 The working group recommends the creation of a mechanism within the WHO to deal with complaints of repression against doctors and attacks against medical ethics.

6 The working group recommends the formulation of a European legal instrument incorporating the European principles of medical ethics adopted by the Meeting of Medical Associations and Councils in January 1987 (Conférence internationale des ordres et des organismes d'attribution similaires).

7 Recalling that Article 7 of the International Covenant on Civil and Political Rights forbids torture and medical and scientific experimentation without the subject's consent, the working group strongly recommends a clarification of the roles of the various bodies concerned with questions of medical ethics and human rights, and also that of pertinent statements.

8 The working group recommends that means be found to improve links between IGOs and NGOs.

9 The working group recommends that medical NGOs play a more active role within IGOs working for the defence and promotion of human rights.

10 The working group recommends improved dissemination of information about the possibilities for action and aid, on an international level, in dealing with violations of human rights.

11 The working group requests medical NGOs to place questions relative to human rights on the agenda of international medical congresses and conferences.

12 The working group urges that appropriate means be instituted to guarantee the professional independence of doctors.

13 The working group asks that doctors be trained so that they are able to examine torture victims adequately.

14 The working group urges medical NGOs to approach the Turkish authorities, particularly via the World Medical Association, urging legal ratification of the draft code of medical ethics drawn up by the Turkish Medical Association.

Working Group 3

Suggested agenda items: Finding a cure for medicine at risk at the national level.

Recommendations
First of all, we were clear that any doctor's involvement in torture strikes at the roots of medical practice. The skills that are given to all health professionals are given for the purpose of healing and the alleviation of suffering. And it is clearly wrong to transmit the technical skills that doctors, nurses and other health professionals have on to any other person without any associated framework of ethics to constrain and limit the way in which those skills are applied.

Now, direct attacks on ethical standards are usually not effective. It was clear to our group that a refusal to compromise in the early stages of an attempt to damage the ethics of a profession is likely to be unsuccessful on the part of the State and can be resisted successfully by the health professionals because at that stage the State is vulnerable to concerted public opposition.

For that reason, it seemed important to us to try to develop indicators which can be applied objectively within a country to determine when the risk of abuse of human rights exists and to try to show this in a way so that doctors, nurses and other health professionals can say an erosion of our professional ethics is taking place. It could be quite difficult to determine when medical ethics, health care ethics, are being eroded because this may be done in a way which is insidious, spread out over a period of time, and máy have the superficial attraction of expediency, even so simple a thing as cost saving to recommend it on the part of the administration.

We found seven indicators, principally to do with care in the prison medical service, because that was the area on which this part of our discussion concentrated. But I emphasise that these are not a complete list. They are only some of the indicators that we found in one particular area and would need to be expanded before they could be regarded as being in any way a comprehensive and useful set of indicators in the national context.

1   First of all, if there is a difference in the standard of care or access to care within prison and outside prison, that would be an indicator that the potential for the abuse of human rights existed. So the quality of care in prison and access to that care should be the same inside the prison population as it is for any population outside the prison.

2   Any death in prison should be the subject of an autopsy, a post mortem examination. And if that is not the case, if regulations do not provide for an autopsy in the case of death in detention, then that is an indicator of the potential for abuse of human rights. We recognised that there are countries or individuals in which, for religious or conscientious reasons, autopsies are not carried out. And remember that we are expressing this as a negative. It may well be that in those countries there is no abuse of human rights. But in the absence of regulations for carrying out autopsies for a death in detention, you should be aware that the potential for the abuse of human rights exists. This creates a burden on the State or on individual members of the profession to prove that the abuse has not occurred.

3   We felt that where a death in detention occurs, if the certificate of death is done by a doctor in the establishment, that too creates a risk and the indicator here that we are looking for, for safety, is that certification of death, where the death has occurred in detention, should be by a medical practitioner who is independent of the establishment.

4   If there are occasions on which treatment is provided by coercion, then that too is an indicator of risk. There may be occasions when, for the safety of the detained persons themselves, that is appropriate, but the burden of proof must then be to show that an abuse of human rights has not occurred. So where there is ever a question of treatment by coercion, that creates the potential for abuse of human rights.

'5   If there are occasions when a doctor or a health professional and a detained person cannot consult in private without the presence of prison guards or police or other people who are extraneous to the consultation, that creates the potential for abuse and is an indicator that should be taken account of.

6   One clear marker for our group was a circumstance in which the health professional was unable to identify himself or herself to a prisoner and where the health professional could not identify the prisoner in the course of a consultation. So, if ever there are circumstances in which a doctor, or health professional, is not permitted to identify himself to a prisoner, or in which the identity is not known to the doctor, that is a very clear marker.

7   Finally, we felt that if research or experimentation was carried out on prisoners, that too should be regarded as indicator of risk for the abuse of human rights. Again, in a similar way to the indicator relating to autopsies, it may be entirely proper in some countries for research to be carried out on the prison population; but once again the burden of proof to show that human rights of prisoners are not being abused then lies with the people who propose to carry out the research or who in fact do that work.

Now these are not glamorous or particularly high-sounding conclusions, nor are the things in the rest of the report that I shall tell you about, but they are some of the small pragmatic actions that will help to construct a barrier to the erosion and destruction of health care ethics. And we felt very strongly that it is these small discrete steps that we need that can be applied both by individual practitioners and by strong independent representative medical organisations in countries.

We have all the international law that we need. We have the Amnesty twelve-point plan. We have international codes of ethics. The problem is not that we need to develop more ethics or more law. The problem is that we need to give individuals the independence and the power to counter the power of the State.

So there were three further areas affecting health professionals that were important. The first is the question of independence and here the key phrase that we have is the necessity for maintaining a distance between the doctors and the State. And this does not just start where we come to questions of abuse of human rights.

It comes to very small mundane things like the questioning of signing a wide range of certificates for all sorts of purposes. Like the question of public health examinations on immigrants coming into the country. Why is this done? For what purpose? If it is done for the purpose of protecting public health, that may be acceptable. If it is done for the purpose of expediting the administration of an immigration policy, that may be quite different. We put an accent on the personal responsibility of the physicians. In particular, we said it is unethical for health professionals to participate in or be present at an execution. We said this prohibition does not preclude a health professional from certifying death, but the certification of death following an execution should occur after a period of time allowing for clinical signs such as rigor mortis, hypothermia and hypostasis. These signs appear only 4 or 5 hours after the extinction of life and will create a clear separation between the doctor's participation in execution which has occurred, and which we wish to stop, and the certification of death.

Finally, we felt it very important that there should be continuing education for doctors on all aspects of medicine and for other health professionals throughout their careers because this tends to create coherence in the profession and is a defence against demands by the State. And we wanted to avoid the isolation of doctors wherever that occurs and that could be done by twinning medical associations not just through international medical organisations but to create particular relationships between two countries so that they can offer mutual support where abuses of human rights may occur.

DR JOHN DAWSON

Working Group 4

Suggested agenda items: ethics, training, and availability of information on medical ethics and human rights.

Recommendations

1 There is a need for basic information on human rights to be made available to all; this should be provided as part of normal schooling so that no one can claim ignorance of human rights issues. There is a need to teach the concept of separation of powers which is the basis of democracy. In countries where there is little formal education, the popular media should be employed (radio, television);

2   Provision of information specifically to health professionals needs to be addressed in two phases:
- at the beginning of studies; this should consist of a review of human rights principles and the discussion of existing medical ethical codes (*not* the creation of new codes);
- at the end of studies, before actively entering into professional life. This should reinforce what has been learned by focusing on situations specific to the daily practice of medicine. This could cover for example: the risks inherent in all situations involving isolation, from the isolation of a dependent elderly person through to the prisoner who is held in incommunicado detention; contact between health professionals and repressive forces: e.g. when and how to say 'no' to the police, for example in a hospital emergency ward; references to examples of extreme situations in countries under repressive governments; joint debates with non-health professionals, e.g. lawyers, community workers, representatives of religious faiths. Such dialogue should underline the joint roles of the lay and scientific communities.

PART THREE: Some texts on medical ethics

UNITED NATIONS PRINCIPLES OF MEDICAL ETHICS (1982)

The principles of medical ethics relevant to the role of health personnel, particularly physicians, in the protection of prisoners and detainees against torture and other cruel, inhuman or degrading treatment or punishment.

Principle 1
Health personnel, particularly physicians, charged with the medical care of prisoners and detainees have a duty to provide them with protection of their physical and mental health and treatment of disease of the same quality and standard as is afforded to those who are not imprisoned or detained.

Principle 2
It is a gross contravention of medical ethics, as well as an offence under applicable international instruments, for health personnel, particularly physicians, to engage, actively or passively, in acts which

constitute participation in, complicity in, incitement to or attempts to commit torture or other cruel, inhuman or degrading treatment or punishment.[1]

Principle 3
It is a contravention of medical ethics for health personnel, particularly physicians, to be involved in any professional relationship with prisoners or detainees the purpose of which is not solely to evaluate, protect or improve their physical and mental health.

Principle 4
It is a contravention of medical ethics for health personnel, particularly physicians:
(a) to apply their knowledge and skills in order to assist in the interrogation of prisoners and detainees in a manner that may adversely affect the physical or mental health or condition of such prisoners or detainees and which is not in accordance with the relevant international instruments;[2]
(b) to certify, or to participate in the certification of, the fitness of prisoners or detainees for any form of treatment or punishment that may adversely affect their physical or mental health and which is not in accordance with the relevant international instruments, or to participate in any way in the infliction of any such treatment or punishment which is not in accordance with the relevant international instruments.

Principle 5
It is a contravention of medical ethics for health personnel, particularly physicians, to participate in any procedure for restraining a prisoner or detainee unless such a procedure is determined in accordance with purely medical criteria as being necessary for the protection of the physical or mental health or the safety of the prisoner or detainee himself, or his fellow-prisoners or detainees, or of his guardians, and presents no hazard to his physical or mental health.

Principle 6
There may be no derogation from the foregoing principles on any grounds whatsoever, including public emergency.

UNITED NATIONS DECLARATION AGAINST TORTURE (1975)

The Declaration on the Protection of all Persons from Torture and other Cruel, Inhuman or Degrading Treatment or Punishment (Declaration against Torture) was adopted without a vote by the United Nations General Assembly on 9 December 1975. It calls upon States to take effective measures to prevent torture and lists some of the most important safeguards and remedies to be provided. It is one of the most important international documents on torture.

Declaration on the protection of all persons from torture and other cruel, inhuman or degrading treatment or punishment

The United Nations General Assembly adopted on 9 December 1975 a Declaration condemning any act of torture or other cruel, inhuman or degrading treatment as 'an offence to human dignity'. Under its terms, no State may permit or tolerate torture or other inhuman or degrading treatment, and each State is requested to take effective measures to prevent such treatment from being practised within its jurisdiction.

The Declaration was first adopted and referred to the Assembly by the Fifth United Nations Congress on the Prevention of Crime and Treatment of Offenders, held in Geneva in September 1975. In adopting the Declaration without a vote, the Assembly noted that the Universal Declaration of Human Rights and the International Covenant on Civil and Political Rights provide that no one may be subjected to torture or to cruel, inhuman or degrading treatment or punishment.

The Assembly has recommended that the Declaration serve as a guideline for all States and other entities exercising effective power.

The text of the Declaration follows:

Article 1

1 For the purpose of this Declaration, torture means any act by which severe pain or suffering, whether physical or mental, is intentionally inflicted by or at the instigation of a public official on a person for such purposes as obtaining from him or a third person information or confession, punishing him for an act he

'has committed or is suspected of having committed, or intimidating him or other persons. It does not include pain or suffering arising only from, inherent in or incidental to, lawful sanctions to the extent consistent with the Standard Minimum Rules for the Treatment of Prisoners.

2 Torture constitutes an aggravated and deliberate form of cruel, inhuman or degrading treatment or punishment.

Article 2

Any act of torture or other cruel, inhuman or degrading treatment or punishment is an offence to human dignity and shall be condemned as a denial of the purposes of the Charter of the United Nations and as a violation of the human rights and fundamental freedoms proclaimed in the Universal Declaration of Human Rights.

Article 3

No State may permit or tolerate torture or other cruel, inhuman or degrading treatment or punishment. Exceptional circumstances such as a state of war or a threat of war, internal political instability or any other public emergency may not be invoked as a justification of torture or other cruel, inhuman or degrading treatment or punishment.

Article 4

Each State shall, in accordance with the provisions of this Declaration, take effective measures to prevent torture and other cruel, inhuman or degrading treatment or punishment from being practised within its jurisdiction.

Article 5

The training of law enforcement personnel and of other public officials who may be responsible for persons deprived of their liberty shall ensure that full account is taken of the prohibition against torture and other cruel, inhuman or degrading treatment or punishment. This prohibition shall also, where appropriate, be included in such general rules or instructions as are issued in regard to the duties and functions of anyone who may be involved in the custody or treatment of such persons.

Article 6

Each State shall keep under systematic review interrogation methods and practices as well as arrangements for the custody and treatment of persons deprived of their liberty in its territory, with a view to preventing any cases of torture or other cruel, inhuman or degrading treatment or punishment.

Article 7
Each State shall ensure that all acts of torture as defined in article 1 are offences under its criminal law. The same shall apply in regard to acts which constitute participation in, complicity in, incitement to or an attempt to commit torture.

Article 8
Any person who alleges that he has been subjected to torture or other cruel, inhuman or degrading treatment or punishment by or at the instigation of a public official shall have the right to complain to, and to have his case impartially examined by, the competent authorities of the State concerned.

Article 9
Wherever there is reasonable ground to believe that an act of torture as defined in article 1 has been committed, the competent authorities of the State concerned shall promptly proceed to an impartial investigation even if there has been no formal complaint.

Article 10
If an investigation under article 8 or article 9 establishes that an act of torture as defined in article 1 appears to have been committed, criminal proceedings shall be instituted against the alleged offender or offenders in accordance with national law. If an allegation of other forms of cruel, inhuman or degrading treatment or punishment is considered to be well founded, the alleged offender or offenders shall be subject to criminal, disciplinary or other appropriate proceedings.

Article 11
Where it is proved that an act of torture or other cruel, inhuman or degrading treatment or punishment has been committed by or at the instigation of a public official, the victim shall be afforded redress and compensation in accordance with national law.

Article 12
Any statement which is established to have been made as a result of torture or other cruel, inhuman or degrading treatment may not

be invoked as evidence against the person concerned or against any other person in any proceedings.

THE WORLD MEDICAL ASSOCIATION TOKYO DECLARATION (1975)

The Tokyo Declaration has, since its adoption in 1975, been the most comprehensive statement produced by the medical profession on the question of the torture and cruel, inhuman or degrading treatment of detainees. It was adopted by the 29th World Medical Assembly, Tokyo, Japan.

The text is as follows:

Tokyo Declaration

It is the privilege of the medical doctor to practise medicine in the service of humanity, to preserve and restore bodily and mental health without distinction as to persons, to comfort and to ease the suffering of his or her patients. The utmost respect for human life is to be maintained even under threat, and no use made of any medical knowledge contrary to the laws of humanity.

For the purpose of this Declaration, torture is defined as the deliberate, systematic or wanton infliction of physical or mental suffering by one or more persons acting alone or on the orders of any authority, to force another person to yield information, to make a confession, or for any other reason.

1 The doctor shall not countenance, condone or participate in the practice of torture or other forms of cruel, inhuman or degrading procedures, whatever the offence of which the victim of such procedures is suspected, accused or guilty, and whatever the victim's beliefs or motives, and in all situations, including armed conflict and civil strife.

2 The doctor shall not provide any premises, instruments, substances or knowledge to facilitate the practice of torture or other forms of cruel, inhuman or degrading treatment or to diminish the ability of the victim to resist such treatment.

3 The doctor shall not be present during any procedure during which torture or other forms of cruel, inhuman or degrading treatment is used or threatened.

4 'A doctor must have complete clinical independence in deciding upon the care of a person for whom he or she is medically responsible. The doctor's fundamental role is to alleviate the distress of his or her fellow-men, and no motive whether personal, collective or political shall prevail against this higher purpose.

5 Where a prisoner refuses nourishment and is considered by the doctor as capable of forming an unimpaired and rational judgment concerning the consequences of such a voluntary refusal of nourishment, he or she shall not be fed artificially. The decision as to the capacity of the prisoner to form such a judgment should be confirmed by at least one other independent doctor. The consequences of the refusal of nourishment shall be explained by the doctor to the prisoner.

6 The World Medical Association will support, and should encourage the international community, the national medical associations and fellow-doctors, to support the doctor and his or her family in the face of threats or reprisals resulting from a refusal to condone the use of torture or other forms of cruel, inhuman or degrading treatment.

RESOLUTION ON PHYSICIAN PARTICIPATION IN CAPITAL PUNISHMENT (WMA, 1981)

Following concern about the introduction of an execution method (lethal injection) which threatened to involve doctors directly in the process of execution, the WMA Secretary-General issued a press statement opposing any involvement of doctors in capital punishment. The 34th Assembly of the WMA, meeting in Lisbon some weeks after the issuing of the press statement, endorsed the Secretary-General's statement in the following terms:

Resolution on physician participation in capital punishment

RESOLVED, that the Assembly of the World Medical Association endorses the action of the Secretary-General in issuing the attached press release on behalf of the World Medical Association condemning physician participation in capital punishment.

FURTHER RESOLVED, that it is unethical for physicians to participate in capital punishment, although this does not preclude physicians certifying death.

FURTHER RESOLVED, that the Medical Ethics Committee keep this matter under active consideration.

Secretary-General's press release

The first capital punishment by intravenous injection of lethal dose of drugs was decided to be carried out next week by the court of the State of Oklahoma, USA.

Regardless of the method of capital punishment a State imposes, no physician should be required to be an active participant. Physicians are dedicated to preserving life.

Acting as an executioner is not the practice of medicine and physician services are not required to carry out capital punishment even if the methodology utilises pharmacological agents or equipment that might otherwise be used in the practice of medicine.

A physician's only role would be to certify death once the State had carried out the capital punishment.

11 September 1981

WORLD PSYCHIATRIC ASSOCIATION
THE HAWAII DECLARATION (1977, 1983)

In early 1976 work commenced on the drafting of an international code of ethics for psychiatrists which was subsequently adopted in 1977 at the VIth World Congress of Psychiatry in Honolulu, Hawaii. At the same meeting the WPA committed itself to receive and investigate allegations of the abuse of psychiatry for political purposes; in 1979 the establishment of the Review Committee was finalised and it first met in Paris in February 1980.

The constitutional status of the Review Committee was changed at the VIIth Congress in Vienna in July 1983 when it was made permanent and had its remit widened.

Minor amendments to the text of the Declaration were agreed at the July 1983 Congress. The text, as amended, reads as follows:

Hawaii Declaration

Ever since the dawn of culture, ethics has been an essential part of the healing art. It is the view of the World Psychiatric Association thát due to conflicting loyalties and expectations of both physicians and patients in contemporary society and the delicate nature of the therapist–patient relationship, high ethical standards are especially important for those involved in the science and practice of psychiatry as a medical speciality. These guidelines have been delineated in order to promote close adherence to those standards and to prevent misuse of psychiatric concepts, knowledge and technology.

Since the psychiatrist is a member of society as well as a practitioner of medicine, he or she must consider the ethical implications specific to psychiatry as well as the ethical demands on all physicians and the social responsibility of every man and woman.

Even though ethical behaviour is based on the individual psychiatrist's conscience and personal judgment, written guidelines are needed to clarify the profession's ethical implications.

Therefore, the General Assembly of the World Psychiatric Association has approved these ethical guidelines for psychiatrists, having in mind the great differences in cultural backgrounds, and in legal, social and economic conditions which exist in the various countries of the world. It should be understood that the World Psychiatric Association views these guidelines to be minimal requirements for ethical standards of the psychiatric profession.

1 The aim of psychiatry is to treat mental illness and to promote mental health. To the best of his or her ability, consistent with accepted scientific knowledge and ethical principles, the psychiatrist shall serve the best interests of the patient and be also concerned for the common good and a just allocation of health resources. To fulfil these aims requires continuous research and continual education of health care personnel, patients and the public.

2 Every psychiatrist should offer to the patient the best available therapy to his knowledge and if accepted must treat him or her with the solicitude and respect due to the dignity of all human beings. When the psychiatrist is responsible for treatment given by others he owes them competent supervision and education. Whenever there is a need, or whenever a reasonable request is forthcoming from the patient, the psychiatrist should seek the help of another colleague.

3 The psychiatrist aspires for a therapeutic relationship that is founded on mutual agreement. At its optimum it requires trust, confidentiality, co-operation and mutual responsibility. Such

' a relationship may not be possible to establish with some patients. In that case, contact should be established with a relative or other person close to the patient. If and when a relationship is established for the purpose other than therapeutic such as in forensic psychiatry, its nature must be thoroughly explained to the person concerned.

4 The psychiatrist should inform the patient of the nature of the condition, therapeutic procedures, including possible alternatives, and of the possible outcome. This information must be offered in a considerate way and the patient must be given the opportunity to choose between appropriate and available methods.

5 No procedure shall be performed nor treatment given against or independent of a patient's own will, unless, because of mental illness, the patient cannot form a judgment as to what is in his or her best interest and without which treatment serious impairment is likely to occur to the patient or others.

6 As soon as the conditions for compulsory treatment no longer apply, the psychiatrist should release the patient from the compulsory nature of the treatment and if further therapy is necessary should obtain voluntary consent. The psychiatrist should inform the patient and/or relatives or meaningful others, of the existence of mechanisms of appeal for the detention and for any other complaints related to his or her well-being.

7 The psychiatrist must never use his professional possibilities to violate the dignity or human rights of any individual or group and should never let inappropriate personal desires, feelings, prejudices or beliefs interfere with the treatment. The psychiatrist must on no account utilise the tools of his profession, once the absence of psychiatric illness has been established. If a patient or some third party demands actions contrary to scientific knowledge or ethical principles, the psychiatrist must refuse to co-operate.

8 Whatever the psychiatrist has been told by the patient, or has noted during examination or treatment, must be kept confidential unless the patient relieves the psychiatrist from this obligation, or to prevent serious harm to self or others makes disclosure necessary. In these cases, however, the patient should be informed of the breach of confidentiality.

9 To increase and propagate psychiatric knowledge and skill requires participation of the patients. Informed consent must, however, be obtained before presenting a patient to a class and,

· if possible, also when a case-history is released for scientific publication, whereby all reasonable measures must be taken to preserve the dignity and anonymity of the patient and to safeguard the personal reputation of the subject. The patient's participation must be voluntary, after full information has been given of the aim, procedures, risks and inconveniences of a research project and there must always be a reasonable relationship between calculated risks or inconveniences and the benefit of the study. In clinical research every subject must retain and exert all his rights as a patient. For children and other patients who cannot themselves give informed consent, this should be obtained from the legal next-of-kin. Every patient or research subject is free to withdraw for any reason at any time from any voluntary treatment and from any teaching or research programme in which he or she participates. This withdrawal, as well as any refusal to enter a programme, must never influence the psychiatrist's efforts to help the patient or subject.

10 The psychiatrist should stop all therapeutic, teaching or research programmes that may evolve contrary to the principles of this Declaration.

INTERNATIONAL COUNCIL OF NURSES

ROLE OF THE NURSE IN THE CARE OF DETAINEES AND PRISONERS (1975)

At the meeting of the Council of National Representatives of the International Council of Nurses in Singapore in August 1975, the following statement was adopted:

Role of the nurse in the care of detainees and prisoners

WHEREAS the ICN Code for Nurses specifically states that:

1 The fundamental responsibility of the nurse is fourfold: to promote health, to prevent illness, to restore health and to alleviate suffering.

2 The nurse's primary responsibility is to those people who require nursing care.

3 The nurse when acting in a professional capacity should at all times maintain standards of personal conduct which reflect credit upon the profession.

4 The nurse takes appropriate action to safeguard the individual when his care is endangered by a co-worker or any other person, and

WHEREAS in 1973 ICN reaffirmed support for the Red Cross Rights and Duties of Nurses under the Geneva Conventions of 1949, which specifically state that, in case of armed conflict of international as well as national character (i.e. internal disorders, civil wars, armed rebellions):

1 Members of the armed forces, prisoners and persons taking no active part in the hostilities
   (a) shall be entitled to protection and care if wounded or sick,
   (b) shall be treated humanely, that is:
       - they may not be subjected to physical mutilation or to medical or scientific experiments of any kind which are not justified by the medical, dental or hospital treatment of the prisoner concerned and carried out in his interest,
       - they shall not be wilfully left without medical assistance and care, nor shall conditions exposing them to contagion or infection be created,
       - they shall be treated humanely and cared for by the Party in conflict in whose power they may be, without adverse distinction founded on sex, race, nationality, religion, political opinion, or any other similar criteria.
2 The following acts are and shall remain prohibited at any time and in any place whatsoever with respect to the above-mentioned persons:
   (a) violence to life and person, in particular murder of all kinds, mutilation, cruel treatment and torture;
   (b) outrages upon personal dignity, in particular humiliating and degrading treatment.

WHEREAS in 1971 ICN endorsed the United Nations Universal Declaration of Human Rights and, hence, accepted that:

1 Everyone is entitled to all the rights and freedoms, set forth in this Declaration, without distinction of any kind, such as race, colour, sex, language, religion, political or other opinion, national or social origin, property, birth or other status (Art. 2),
2 No one shall be subjected to torture or to cruel, inhuman or degrading treatment or punishment (Art. 5); and

WHEREAS in relation to detainees and prisoners of conscience, interrogation procedures are increasingly being employed which result in ill-effects, often permanent, on the person's mental and physical health;

THEREFORE BE IT RESOLVED that ICN condemns the use of all such procedures harmful to the mental and physical health of prisoners and detainees; and

FURTHER BE IT RESOLVED that nurses having knowledge of physical or mental ill-treatment of detainees and prisoners take appropriate action including reporting the matter to appropriate national and/or international bodies; and

FURTHER BE IT RESOLVED that nurses participate in clinical research carried out on prisoners, only if the freely given consent of the patient has been secured after a complete explanation and understanding by the patient of the nature and risk of the research; and

FINALLY BE IT RESOLVED that the nurse's first responsibility is towards her patients, notwithstanding considerations of national security and interest.

STATEMENT ON THE NURSE'S ROLE IN SAFEGUARDING HUMAN RIGHTS (1983)

Responding to requests from national member associations for guidance on the protection of human rights of both nurses and those for whom they care, the Council of National Representatives of the International Council of Nurses adopted the statement given below at its meeting in Brasilia in June 1983.

Statement on the nurse's role in safeguarding human rights

This document has been developed in response to the requests of national nurses' associations for guidance in assisting nurses to safeguard their own human rights and those for whom they have professional responsibility. It is meant to be used in conjunction with the ICN Code for Nurses and resolutions relevant to human rights. Nurses should also be familiar with the Geneva Conventions and the additional protocols as they relate to the responsibilities of nurses.

The current world situation is such that there are innumerable circumstances in which a nurse may become involved that require action on her/his part to safeguard human rights. Nurses are accountable for their own professional actions and must therefore be clear as to what is expected of them in such situations.

Also conflict situations have increased in number and often include internal political upheaval, and strife, or international war. The nature of war is changing. Increasingly nurses find themselves having to act or respond in complex situations to which there seems to be no clear-cut solution.

Changes in the field of communications also have increased the awareness and sensitivity of all groups to those conflict situations.

The need for nursing actions to safeguard human rights is not restricted to times of political upheaval and war. It can also arise in prisons or in the normal work situation of any nurse where abuse of patients, nurses, or others is witnessed or suspected. Nurses have a responsibility in each of these situations to take action to safeguard the rights of those involved. Physical abuse and mental abuse are equally of concern to the nurse. Over- or under-treatment is another area to be watched. There may be pressures applied to use one's knowledge and skills in ways that are not beneficial to patients or others.

Scientific discoveries have brought about more sophisticated forms of torture and methods of resuscitation so that those being tortured can be kept alive for repeated sessions. It is in such circumstances that nurses must be clear about what actions they must take as in no way can they participate in such torture, or torture techniques.

Nurses have individual responsibility but often they can be more effective if they approach human rights issues as a group. The national nurses' associations need to ensure that their structure provides a realistic mechanism through which nurses can seek confidential advice, counsel, support and assistance in dealing with these difficult situations. Verification of the facts reported will be an important first step in any particular situation.

At times it will be appropriate for the NNA to become a spokesman for the nurses involved. They may also be required to negotiate for them. It is *essential* that confidentiality be maintained. In rare cases the personal judgment of the nurse may be such that other actions seem more appropriate than approaching the Association.

The nurse initiating the actions requires knowledge of her own and others' human rights, moral courage, a well thought through plan of action and a commitment and determination to see that the necessary follow-up does occur. Personal risk is a factor that has to be considered and each person must use her/his best judgment in the situation.

Rights of those in need of care
– Health care is a right of all individuals. Everyone should have access to health care regardless of financial, political, geographic, racial or religious considerations. The nurse should seek to ensure such impartial treatment.
– Nurses must ensure that adequate treatment is provided – within available resources – and in accord with nursing ethics (ICN Code) to all those in need of care.
– A patient/prisoner has the right to refuse to eat or to refuse treatments. The nurse may need to verify that the patient/prisoner understands the implications of such action but she should not participate in the administration of food or medications to such patients.

Rights and duties of nurses
– When considering the rights and duties of nursing personnel it needs to be remembered that both action and lack of action can have a detrimental effect and the nursing personnel must be considered accountable on both counts.
– Nurses have a right to practise within the code of ethics and nursing legislation of the country in which they practise. Personal safety – freedom from abuse, threats or intimidation – is the right of every nurse.
– National nurses' associations have a responsibility to participate in development of health and social legislation relative to patients' rights and all related topics.
– It *is a duty* to have informed consent of patients relative to having research done on them and in receiving treatments such as blood transfusions, anaesthesia, grafts etc. Such informed consent is a patient's right and must be ensured.

AMNESTY INTERNATIONAL Twelve-Point Programme for the Prevention of Torture (Adopted in October 1983)

Torture is a fundamental violation of human rights, condemned by the General Assembly of the United Nations as an offence to human dignity and prohibited under national and international law.

Yet torture persists, daily and across the globe. In Amnesty International's experience, legislative prohibition is not enough. Immediate steps are needed to confront torture and other cruel, inhuman or degrading treatment or punishment wherever they occur and to eradicate them totally.

Amnesty International calls on all governments to implement the following Twelve-Point Programme for the Prevention of Torture. It invites concerned individuals and organisations to join in promoting the programme. Amnesty International believes that the implementation of these measures is a positive indication of a government's commitment to abolish torture and to work for its abolition worldwide.

1 Official condemnation of torture

The highest authorities of every country should demonstrate their total opposition to torture. They should make clear to all law-enforcement personnel that torture will not be tolerated under any circumstances.

2 Limits on incommunicado detention

Torture often takes place while the victims are held incommunicado – unable to contact people outside who could help them or find out what is happening to them. Governments should adopt safeguards to ensure that incommunicado detention does not become an opportunity for torture. It is vital that all prisoners be brought before a judicial authority promptly after being taken into custody and that relatives, lawyers and doctors have prompt and regular access to them.

3 No secret detention

In some countries torture takes place in secret centres, often after the victims are made to 'disappear'. Governments should ensure that prisoners are held in publicly recognised places, and that accurate information about their whereabouts is made available to relatives and lawyers.

4 Safeguards during interrogation and custody

Governments should keep procedures for detention and interrogation under regular review. All prisoners should be promptly told of their rights, including the right to lodge complaints about their treatment. There should be regular independent visi.3 of inspection to places of detention. An important safeguard against torture would be the separation of authorities responsible for detention from those in charge of interrogation.

5   Independent investigation of reports of torture

Governments should ensure that all complaints and reports of torture are impartially and effectively investigated. The methods and findings of such investigations should be made public. Complainants and witnesses should be protected from intimidation.

6   No use of statements extracted under torture

Governments should ensure that confessions or other evidence obtained through torture may never be invoked in legal proceedings.

7   Prohibition of torture in law

Governments should ensure that acts of torture are punishable offences under the criminal law. In accordance with international law, the prohibition of torture must not be suspended under any circumstances, including states of war or other public emergency.

8   Prosecution of alleged torturers

Those responsible for torture should be brought to justice. This principle should apply wherever they happen to be, wherever the crime was committed and whatever the nationality of the perpetrators or victims. There should be no 'safe haven' for torturers.

9   Training procedures

It should be made clear during the training of all officials involved in the custody, interrogation or treatment of prisoners that torture is a criminal act. They should be instructed that they are obliged to refuse to obey any order to torture.

10   Compensation and rehabilitation

Victims of torture and their dependants should be entitled to obtain financial compensation. Victims should be provided with appropriate medical care or rehabilitation.

11 *International response*

Governments should use all available channels to intercede with governments accused of torture. Inter-governmental mechanisms should be established and used to investigate reports of torture urgently and to take effective action against it. Governments should ensure that military, security or police transfers or training do not facilitate the practice of torture.

12 *Ratification of international instruments*

All governments should ratify international instruments containing safeguards and remedies against torture, including the International Covenant on Civil and Political Rights and its Optional Protocol which provides for individual complaints.

The Twelve-Point Programme was adopted by Amnesty International in October 1983 as part of the organisation's Campaign for the Abolition of Torture.

Notes

1. See the Declaration on the Protection of All Persons from Being Subjected to Torture and Other Cruel, Inhuman or Degrading Treatment or Punishment (General Assembly Resolution 3452 [XXX], annex), article 1 of which can be found on p. 147.
   Article 7 of the Declaration can be found on p. 148.
2. Particularly the Universal Declaration of Human Rights (General Assembly resolution 217 A [III]), the International Covenants on Human Rights (General Assembly resolution 2200 A [XXI], annex), the Declaration on the Protection of all Persons from Being Subjected to Torture and Other Cruel, Inhuman or Degrading Treatment or Punishment (General Assembly resolution 3452 [XXX], annex) and the Standard Minimum Rules for the Treatment of Prisoners (First United Nations Congress on the Prevention of Crime and the Treatment of Offenders: report by the Secretariat [United Nations publication, Sales No. 1956. IV. 4], annex I.A.).

Post-script

Since the date of the seminar on which this book is based, there have been a number of developments in the field of torture and the death penalty:

WORLD PSYCHIATRIC ASSOCIATION

1 *Declaration on the Participation of Psychiatrists in the Death Penalty*, adopted at the 8th World Congress, Athens, October, 1989.

Psychiatrists are physicians and adhere to the Hippocratic Oath 'to practice for the good of patients and never to do harm'. The World Psychiatric Association is an international association with 77 member societies.

CONSIDERING that the United Nations' Principles of Medical Ethics enjoins physicians – and thus psychiatrists – to refuse to enter into any relationship with a prisoner other than one directed at evaluating, protecting or improving their physical and mental health, and further

CONSIDERING that the Declaration of Hawaii of the WPA resolves that the psychiatrist shall serve the best interests of the patient with the solicitude and respect due to the dignity of all human beings and that the psychiatrist must refuse to co-operate if some third party demands actions contrary to ethical principles,

CONSCIOUS that psychiatrists may be called upon to participate in any action connected to executions,

DECLARES that the participation of psychiatrists in any such action is a violation of professional ethics.

2 Provisional return of the USSR to membership of the WPA, agreed at the 8th World Congress in October, 1989.

AMNESTY INTERNATIONAL

The *Declaration on the Participation of Health Personnel in the Death Penalty*, first formulated in 1981, was modified in 1988 in the light of developments on the issue:

DECLARES that the participation of health personnel in executions is a violation of professional ethics;
CALLS UPON health personnel not to participate in executions;
FURTHER CALLS UPON organisations of health professionals:
- to protect health professionals who refuse to participate in executions
- to adopt resolutions to these ends, and
- to promote worldwide adherence to these standards.

BRITISH MEDICAL ASSOCIATION

A working party is at present preparing a report on the role of the doctor in torture, judicial execution, amputation, flogging, etc. It will be more comprehensive than their TORTURE REPORT, 1986, and is expected to be available in late 1991.

INSTITUTE OF MEDICAL ETHICS

A working party on medical involvement in torture has been set up under the chairmanship of Sir Raymond Hoffenberg. It will consider, *inter alia*, the means whereby doctors in those countries where torture is practised can be helped to resist participation.

INTERNATIONAL COUNCIL OF NURSES

1 *Position Statement on Nurses and Torture*, adopted in Seoul, May, 1989.

The Responsibility of the Nurse
The nurse shall not countenance, condone or voluntarily participate in:
Any deliberate, systematic or wanton infliction of physical or mental suffering or any other form of cruel, inhuman or degrading procedure by any one or more persons acting alone or on the orders of any authority, to force another person to yield information, to make confession, or for any other reason;
Any treatment which denies to any person the respect which is his/her due as a human being.

2 *The Death Penalty and Participation by Nurses in Executions*, adopted in Seoul, May, 1989.

The Responsibility of the Nurse
RESOLVES that the International Council of Nurses considers participation by nurses, either directly or indirectly, in the immediate preparation for and the carrying out of state authorised executions to be a violation of nursing's ethical code; and further
RESOLVES that the International Council of Nurses urges its member associations to work for the abolishment of the death penalty in all those countries still practising this form of punishment.

UNITED NATIONS

The Convention on the Rights of the Child, adopted in November, 1989, sets out in Article 37:

Torture and deprivation of liberty.
The prohibition of torture, cruel treatment or punishment, capital punishment, life imprisonment and unlawful arrest or deprivation of liberty. The principles of appropriate treatment, separation from detained adults, contact with family and access to legal and other assistance.